Months of Moments of Bliss

The Biography of Hampshire trainer
Bill Wightman

ALAN YUILL WALKER

A & V Publishing
Lambourn

To Eileen Barling

Cover photograph by Edward Whitaker

Copyright © Alan Yuill Walker, 1995

Published in Great Britain by
A & V Publishing
Sheepdrove Park, Lambourn,
Berkshire RG17 7UN

All rights reserved. No part of this publication may be reproduced, stored in a retrieval system, or transmitted, in any form or by any means, electronic, mechanical, photocopying, recording or otherwise, without the prior permission of the copyright owner.

ISBN No. 0-9526844-0-3

Typeset and printed by Manns Printers
Tel: 01638 711142

CONTENTS

Foreword iv
Preface v

1 Born and brought up in London 1
2 Getting started as a Trainer 7
3 A Japanese Prisoner of War 14
4 Back in Harness 20
5 Heartbreak on the Gallops 25
6 A new Stable Star 30
7 The Renewal of a great Partnership 40
8 Other prominent Jumpers 47
9 Two Lady Owner-Breeders 53
10 The M.P. who bought the National Stud 64
11 More big Handicap Successes 71
12 Some old Stalwarts 86
13 Homebred Winners 96
14 Reflections on a Trainer's Life 102
15 A Team Effort 110
16 The longest serving Trainer 117

Photographs 73
Chronological List of Winners 121

Foreword

I was fortunate enough to have Bill Wightman as my original trainer - he trained my first horse Cathy Jane to win the Brown Jack Stakes at Ascot in 1973.

Our association dates back to the days of Flying Nelly, Somersway, Privateer, Solar and many others, when, as a footballer playing only a few miles down the road at Southampton, I took every opportunity to get up on the gallops. It was always a pleasure to visit Upham to see my own and the other horses - Bill always had some story to tell or theory to pass on which I found fascinating.

I shall always remember one occasion when Man on the Run, the first foal out of Cathy Jane, ran at Bath. Half of Southampton Football Club were in the stands having had the inevitable few quid on and gave the horse suitable verbal encouragement. He won and as I walked into the winner's enclosure, Bill said, "I found out something about your horse today, Mick. "What's that?" I asked. "He loves to be shouted at!"

Everyone in the business knows Bill to be a gentleman and a true professional. In my opinion he ranks as one of the best trainers of the last thirty to forty years. He was the shrewdest placer of horses, winning all the big handicaps - which most of the bookmakers know to their cost. He also had the ability to train anything from a 5 furlong sprinter to a 2 mile stayer, not to mention the 'chasers.

I consider myself very privileged to have been associated with Bill, not only as an owner, but also as a fellow trainer, and above all I value his enthusiasm and love for his horses which have been so infectious and an inspiration to me.

Mick Channon
Upper Lambourn

Preface

Getting started as a racehorse trainer, which is a precarious occupation at the best of times, is never easy. Trainers invariably fall into one of two categories - they either have sufficient private means to enable them to start without having to rely on training fees as their primary source of income, or they have made a name for themselves in the racing world as a jockey, either professional or amateur. A fortunate minority inherit a stable - others go as someone's assistant and then take over upon that trainer's retirement. Alternatively they may have a farm and progress from the ranks of point-to-points and hunter-chases.

The career of Bill Wightman, who is the only man living to have been training before the Second World War and to have saddled a winner on the new all weather tracks, represents a remarkable success story from an unfavourable draw, for he started without any of the more obvious advantages. Instead he got himself on the first rung of the ladder by training under Pony Turf Club Rules, thus making full use of the only opportunity available. It is an unique accomplishment spanning sixty years during which time he proved equally proficient with jumpers as on the flat - a very rare achievement amongst the training ranks.

He trained his first winner, under National Hunt Rules in May 1937, aged twenty-two, and his first under Jockey Club Rules that September. The last of more than 700 winners came at the age of seventy-nine in October 1993 - and no sooner had he officially 'retired' than he was saddling winners in point-to-points. Small wonder he has long been recognised in the business as the 'professional's professional', and there is no greater compliment than that. The great Findon trainer Ryan Price, who was not given to lavishing praise on his colleagues, is on record as saying that W.G.R. Wightman was at the very top of his profession.

But Bill Wightman was never leading trainer and he never saddled a Classic winner. A trainer of the old school, he trained mostly for friends and 'small' owners and that meant either buying cheap yearlings or taking homebreds from low budget breeding operations whose connections invariably regarded their geese as swans. Ask him what his greatest training achievement was, and he says, "probably winning a seller with an unsound animal." And he nominates the gelded Tracklecka, who won sellers at Bath and Newmarket, as just such a plater. He also emphasises how imperative it is to have owners who are good at paying their bills!

During his long innings, he trained a handful of top horses under both Rules of whom Halloween, that charismatic three-mile 'chaser of the 1950s, stands head and shoulders above everything else in terms of class. The great majority of the inmates, first at Dean Farm, Bishop's Waltham, and then at Ower Farm, Upham, were run-of-the-mill animals with no aspirations to competing in what are termed nowadays as Pattern Races. His lasting testimonial is that he managed to train the winners of just about every major handicap in *The Racing Calendar* and no one achieves that without skill and dedication.

The art of training is the ability to place horses to their best advantage and no one could do that better than Bill Wightman, who adds, "preferably without it being too obvious to the handicapper!" Not that he was ever found guilty of contravening Rule 151 which is concerned with horses running on their merits. Certainly his homebred filly Googly was an appropriate winner to bow out with as she finished in the frame in seven of her thirteen runs that season! And he knew the time of day; not many of those winners went unbacked by the stable, although to call him a betting trainer would give entirely the wrong impression.

What describes him best is a complete master of his craft. A man of old fashioned modesty and charm, he has always had a twinkle in his eye and a ready sense of humour. Never one to take himself too seriously, he regarded the prospect of having a biography written about him as rather daunting, and the reality as extremely flattering. For the author, whose first insight into racing behind the scenes was being taken round evening stables by Bill Wightman nearly forty-five years ago, it has been a most rewarding journey down memory lane.

The task was made that much easier by Bill Wightman's unfailing hospitality and patience, not to mention his amazing memory for detail about a sport which he has enriched for so long. "Quite simply it has been my life", he says, "and it has been a privilege to train other people's horses." Fortunately there are those who still appreciate old world courtesies and nothing pleased the master of Ower Farm more on finally relinquishing his licence than to receive a charming letter from the then Senior Steward of the Jockey Club, Lord Hartington, wishing him well in his retirement. It is a sentiment with which all in racing would concur.

Alan Yuill Walker
Lambourn

1
Born and brought up in London

It is rather a coincidence that the biography of William Gilbert Rowell Wightman should be published in 1995. During the year three totally unrelated occurrences made the headlines and all of them have a striking relevance for this retired, senior trainer of racehorses from Upham in Hampshire. They are the 50th anniversary of VJ Day at the end of the Second World War with all the agonising memories that that engenders; the astonishing collapse of Barings Bank, the oldest established merchant bank in the City; and the exceptional prowess of Dulwich College's under-15s rugby side, which won the schools' final for their age group at Twickenham.

Born in Streatham, London, SW16, on July 9, 1914, Bill Wightman was educated locally at Dulwich College, having attended the prep school there. He was also a Japanese prisoner of war for three-and-a-half years as a young gunnery officer, first in Java, then in Singapore and finally in Borneo. Furthermore, it was largely through the financial support of Evelyn Baring, a member of the banking dynasty, that he was able to pursue his ambition of becoming a racehorse trainer. Remarkably for someone born and brought up in suburbia, Bill always had a love of horses which he says he inherited from his father, also William - he followed Bill's training career with great interest until he died in his 90th year.

Months of Misery Moments of Bliss

Bill regards himself as a Scotsman who just happened to be born in London - his father came from Edinburgh and his mother from the Shetland Islands. "I remember my father saying that all he ever wanted to do was to work in the Royal Botanical Gardens in Edinburgh." But that did not meet with parental approval, so he went abroad, first to Canada in about 1898, and then to South Africa at the time of the Boer War, staying in Cape Town with his sister who was married to a surgeon. The family owned a business in Edinburgh selling sheet music and for a period William Wightman worked as a piano tuner, although at the time his son was born he was an insurance inspector.

Music and the arts run in Bill's immediate family. His mother was a talented painter of miniatures - as Winifred Ursula Nicolson, her work was exhibited at The Royal Academy and at The Hermitage. Her grandfather had been the minister at Unst and Yell in the Shetlands, but she was born in St. Petersburg, her father having gone to Russia to work for the British and Foreign Bible Society. However, she was educated in Edinburgh and as a young girl, together with her elder sisters, used to travel to and from St. Petersburg on board the timber ships which regularly plied the North Sea from Russia to London's Hay's Wharf. She also studied art at Edinburgh University and it seems likely that this was where she first met her future husband.

At school Bill excelled at all ball games. However, he was never any good at running, unlike fellow Alleynian, Geoffrey Hamlyn, the doyen of the betting ring who was captain of athletics. Sport certainly took precedence over everything else, and in view of the financial sacrifices his parents made in sending him to Dulwich, he regrets having never passed any examinations such was his preoccupation with playing games. Cricket was his particular forte and he was wicket keeper for the best XI that Dulwich College ever fielded. Also in the team was S.C. (Billy) Griffith who was to keep wicket for Sussex and the MCC of which he became secretary. All of which goes

Born and brought up in London

some way to explaining just how good a cricketer W.G.R. Wightman really was.

"My form master in the lower IVth was a medium pace spin bowler called C.S. 'Doggy' Marriott, who played for Kent and was very tall," Bill recalls. "As wicket keepers, he used to make us stand up right behind the batsman - we were only allowed to stand back to ultra fast bowlers - nowadays they stand back to medium fast bowlers and we had none of the elaborate protection they have, just a box and ordinary pads and gloves. Originally my father taught me to play all games as he did my sisters - they were both good tennis players and qualified for junior Wimbledon. My elder sister, who is four years my senior, still plays golf."

Just eighteen when he left Dulwich, Bill took a job as an office junior at £1-10s-0d a week, working for the Wheat Commission in Smith's Square, Westminster - the government had just started paying a subsidy to farmers for growing wheat. "We actually received £1-8s-6d, the remaining 1s-6d paying for our insurance stamp. I commuted from home and the tram fare was 6s per week. Sandwiches for lunch cost 6d per day! A packet of 20 cigarettes cost 11½d and a gallon of petrol was 11d!"

Bill had enjoyed the OTC (Officers' Training Corps) at school, particularly the shooting at Bisley, and one of the first things he did on leaving Dulwich was to join the Yeomanry, the mounted section of the Territorials, as a trooper. "They had a riding school at the Duke of York's Barracks, just off Sloane Square, where we had to parade once a week. We used to go to Knightsbridge to ride the Household Cavalry horses and there were summer camps at places like Findon and Michel Grove in Sussex. During a fortnight's camp there was always the opportunity to ride the officers' chargers."

One of Bill's favourite occupations during the school holidays had been to cycle down to Croydon aerodrome as he had a fascination for flying. But he also did a certain amount of riding and had been racing locally at Epsom and at various point-to-points in the south. On balance he became more enamoured with horses than aeroplanes, and was soon contemplating a career in racing. But how to set about it? The trouble was that he had always been told it was impossible to effect an entree into the world of racing without some sort of family connections and he had none. And there certainly wasn't enough money to enable him to ride as an amateur. But as luck would have it, he was destined to meet two Old Etonians, Geoffrey Gilbey and Evelyn Baring, who with a shared interest in racing, made the whole thing possible.

Chance is a fine thing and had Bill not acccepted an invitation to play a little country house cricket, he would probably never have met either Geoffrey Gilbey or Evelyn Baring. Not long after leaving Dulwich, he was on holiday in Sussex when he received a telegram from an ex contemporary in the school team asking whether he would keep wicket for Geoffrey Gilbey's XI. The week ended with a match against the Eton Manor Boys' Club at Hackney Wick. "On the Saturday Geoffrey Gilbey took us all racing at Hurst Park and I won £13-10s-0d. I'll never forget it because on the way home I bought a bull-nose Morris car for £7-10s-0d out of the winnings." How well he remembers turning up for work in his new acquisition!

The doyen of racing journalists, Geoffrey Gilbey (1889-1969), a member of the celebrated drinks' family, was a man of deep religious conviction. Always anxious to help the young and needy, he expended a tremendous amount of time, energy and money on assisting those less fortunate than himself. His uncle Sir Walter Gilbey was a racing enthusiast and so were two of Geoffrey's brothers. The eldest, Ronald, who ran the family business, had horses in training in Belgium, while Quintin also became a distinguished member of the racing press.

Having a horse in training with Laing Ward, outside Winchester, was strictly in keeping with Geoffrey Gilbey's idea of sporting fun - whilst up at Oxford he had gained a Blue for athletics and well into middle age he enjoyed nothing more than organising and playing in his own cricket XI. On coming down from Christ Church he considered entering the Church, but instead decided to work in the theatre. Always a keen music lover, he composed a marching song which was later adopted by the Rifle Brigade battalion in which he served as a young man in France and Belgium during the First World War.

In 1919 he joined the *Sunday Express* as a racing reporter and writing about racing became his principal occupation throughout the remainder of his working life. He was the first racing journalist to broadcast a commentary on a race and it was he who persuaded Lord Beaverbrook to take Clive Graham on to the staff of the *Daily Express*. Another memorable occasion was being interviewed on ITV at Sandown Park in March 1960 and when asked for selections for the remaining five races, promptly gave all five winners!

During the Second World War, Geoffrey, who is commemorated by a 'chase at Newbury's March fixture, organised and commanded a special training unit for soldiers 'in trouble'. Back in Civvie Street he helped to find jobs for first offenders when they left prison and was closely involved with the Federation of Boys' Clubs. He also concerned himself with the welfare of former racehorses and worked in conjunction with the ILPH (International League for the Protection of Horses), and the affiliated Ada Cole Memorial Home for Horses, to improve their lot on retirement, particularly those shipped overseas for slaughter.

It was through their joint involvement with the Eton Manor Boys' Club, which was founded in the early part of the century at Hackney Wick, that Geoffrey Gilbey and Evelyn Baring became close friends. The Eton Manor Boys' Club played a very significant part in Evelyn Baring's life (1893-1966). For twelve years prior to the last war he lived in the Manor House attached to the club building, an association he maintained until he died. His particular interest was the swimming section, the Eton Otters, of which he was president for more than thirty years.

Months of Misery Moments of Bliss

Evelyn Baring was a prominent member of the family merchant bank. He first became a director in 1923 and was an executive director until he retired aged seventy. During the War he served in the RAF and was a member of the team of eminent businessmen co-opted by Lord Beaverbrook to get things done. Beneath a light hearted exterior were the qualities of flair and shrewdness which enabled him to make his mark in the City - he was associated with many ingenious deals between the Argentine Government and British investors and not long before his death was closely involved in supporting Courtaulds against the ICI takeover. Bill remembers Evelyn Baring as a very dutiful son who seldom missed coming down in his Bentley at weekends to visit his mother at her Brockenhurst home in the New Forest.

Meanwhile Bill had kept in contact with Geoffrey Gilbey through cricket. One day he told him that he had rather a dead end office job 'licking stamps' and was anxious to get involved in racing in some capacity or another. "If Geoffrey couldn't do you a good turn he certainly wouldn't do you a bad one," says Bill. "It was upon his suggestion that I went to work for his trainer Laing Ward, near Headbourne Worthy, north of Winchester, just to see how I liked it." And that was the catalyst that sparked off his long career as a racehorse trainer.

2
Getting started as a Trainer

Bill Wightman was still only eighteen when he joined Laing Ward near Headbourne Worthy where his gallops were on the site of the old Winchester Racecourse. As a working student he did his two horses like any other lad in the yard. "Laing Ward had built some wooden boxes in some beautiful country at South Wonston beside the RAF aerodrome which housed those huge Virginia Bombers," he recalls. "The amazing thing is that his son Frank, who is about my age, couldn't bear to leave the place and is still there running a riding school called Cloudbank."

That establishment takes its name from the 1925 Goodwood Cup winner who was one of Laing Ward's best horses when he was private trainer to the notorious gambler Jimmy White at Foxhill. This was just down the road from White's weekend home King Edward's Place, high on the Berkshire Downs close to Lambourn. By the time White committed suicide two years later Ward had moved from Stanton in Shropshire, where he was private trainer to Mr J. Reid Walker, to Shrewton in Wiltshire. Then in December 1928 he set up as a public trainer near Headbourne Worthy. Laing Ward died there in May 1944, having retired from training a few months after the outbreak of War. It was from an adjacent yard that Tommy Rayson sent out

Months of Misery Moments of Bliss

Lovely Cottage to win the 1946 Grand National for John Morant, father of the present senior starter Simon Morant.

It soon became evident that Bill was not only an excellent rider, but also had a natural rapport with horses. Within a year he was presented with an unexpected proposition: would he take charge of a small string of ponies owned by Geoffrey Gilbey and his friends to race at Northolt Park in Middlesex? Although pony racing was not exactly de rigueur, Northolt was recognised as one of the best appointed courses in the country - indeed the amenities there for the general public were far ahead of anywhere else. There was racing at Northolt every Saturday and Monday from the middle of March to the beginning of November with evening meetings, the first in England, on Wednesdays during the summer. There was also pony racing nearer to Headbourne Worthy at Portsmouth Park.

Gilbey's ponies were stabled at Cloudbank. Bill took over there in November 1933 with the assistance of Frank Ward and Bob Emery, whose father had been a jockey and trainer in Austria-Hungary. The team made a brilliant start, sending out no less than twenty-two winners that first season - the best of them was Geoffrey Gilbey's Another Chance, winner of the prestigious Northolt Cup, who had been bought out of a seller earlier that season for 125 guineas. He was ridden by John Every who lived at Newmarket and combined his duties as a trial jockey for Lord Ellesmere with pony racing. Modestly Bill describes such a golden run of success as 'beginner's luck'. But obviously he had learnt well during his time with Laing Ward who was an expert in placing his mostly moderate horses to the best advantage.

"Up till then there had been no outlet for small thoroughbreds," explains Bill. "The big trainers used to get all their small two-year-olds ready early on, however well bred they were, to run in maidens and sellers at all the early meetings. This provided a wonderful opportunity for me as we used to buy anything that came on the market. To qualify for racing under Pony Turf Club Rules the ponies had to be 15

Getting started as a Trainer

hands or under. In fact all the two-year-olds we bought managed to win. It was a case of every new arrival would gallop up Worthy Down beating those we already had. Some of them were beautifully bred but the big stables had to get rid of them somewhere. I remember two who came from Fred Darling at Beckhampton and one of them, a Coronach filly, was an absolute so and so."

His very first pony winner was the four-year-old Swift Mary (Forerunner - Mary Selby), who was bred by Lord Wavertree, the man who presented the National Stud at Tully to the British nation. Swift Mary was one of a group of ponies that Bill took during the winter months to work on the sands at Studland Bay near the entrance to Poole Harbour. "We took them over on the ferry which chugged across on chains from Sandbanks and stabled them in a yard adjacent to the Knoll House Hotel. We went there some time after Christmas and I think it probably gave them a fitness edge. There's nothing new in this game you know!" It was on the beach at Sandbanks that Mrs. Louie Dingwall, one of racing's great characters, used to train her small string.

Another successful pony, the wall-eyed Lavinia Gray (Duncan Gray - Young Lavinia), had been homebred by Mrs Lionel Corbett who was to become one of Bill's neighbours when he moved to Upham. Mrs Corbett, who had horses in training with Ossie Bell in Lambourn, was the daughter of Sir Richard Garton. He raced that top sprinter Sir Cosmo and bought Brook Stud, Newmarket, specifically to stand the horse. Later her son John Corbett owned the Bill Wightman trained Halview Pet in partnership with Herbert Blagrave, this King Hal mare scoring on her debut over hurdles at Newbury.

All the while pony racing was gaining in esteem and popularity with the involvement of a number of big names. The leading combination was Dorothy Paget (owner), Pat Donoghue (trainer), and Tommy Carey (jockey). However, Bill's aim had always been to get into racing proper. The big breakthrough came on May 18, 1937, when he saddled Mr

Months of Misery Moments of Bliss

G.H. Rumsey's Sunny Peace (Orb - Break the Peace), to score in the £58 Devonshire 'Chase at Buckfastleigh ridden by the young professional Bruce Hobbs; the following year aged seventeen on Battleship, he became the youngest rider ever to win the Grand National. Twelve-year-old Sunny Peace scored by fifteen lengths from the evens favourite, the remaining three runners all falling. The old gelding, who had been fired, had been bought for just 50 guineas after winning a seller at Fontwell Park the previous month by his owner who had lost both his legs in the First World War.

That September Bill saddled his first winner on the flat when his own six-year-old gelding Autumn (Stefan the Great - Spring III), won the £107 Willoughby (Amateur Riders') Plate at Warwick over 11 furlongs, partnered by Peter Herbert. "I had picked out the worst race I could find to suit a big, strong horse. I made the entry and promptly sent a telegram to Quinny Gilbey asking him to ride which gave him something to flash about the press room! He wired back 'regret unable to accept, but have obtained services of next best available!' "

Bought privately for £25 from Tommy Rayson, Autumn had had a chequered career. He had been tubed and had shown an aversion to jumping. Bill describes him as a 'ladies' horse'. Coincidentally, Autumn had at one time been owned, like Sunny Peace, by James V. Rank, the flour miller. However, during his first three seasons he had been trained at Newmarket by Cecil Boyd-Rochfort for his American patron Joe Widener for whom he scored six victories, all in the hands of Joe Childs. As a young trainer Bill once asked Joe Childs to ride for him but the great jockey declined the invitation with the explanation, 'I never ride on Mondays!'

Whereas Geoffrey Gilbey helped to put Bill Wightman on the road to success as a trainer of ponies at South Wonston where both Sunny Peace and Autumn were trained, it was really Evelyn Baring who provided the wherewithal for him to make the transition to the world of 'real racehorses' as in 1937 he bought Dean Farm, Bishop's Waltham, between Winchester

Getting started as a Trainer

and Southampton. This was part of Sir Harry Warden Chilcott's estate, centred on the neighbouring village of Upham. "I remember Evelyn Baring telephoning me to say there was going to be a war and that he was keen to buy a farm. When he decided on purchasing the farm, he was delighted that it included some gallops and he immediately asked me if I would like to train there. So at the end of the season I moved from South Wonston to Dean which like all the other farms on the estate at that time was in a pretty derelict state."

Warden Chilcott, who had first registered his racing colours in 1904, was knighted in 1922 for services to politics. Equally keen on yachting as on racing and breeding, he had been MP for the Walton Division of Liverpool from 1918 to 1929 and had served as a Lt-Commander in the Royal Naval Air Service during the Great War. He also owned a castle at St. Florent in Corsica, where he hunted wild boar, and the Hook Estate bordering Southampton Water. Adjacent to his home Salterns at Warsash, the Hook Estate included a private aerodrome and an eighteen-hole golf course.

Dean was one of four farms on the Upham estate, the others being Woodcote Farm, Ower Farm and Street End Farm, with Stephen's Castle Down conveniently placed at the centre. Evelyn Baring procured Street End Farm prior to Warden Chilcott's death (Bill remembers them haymaking there during the War before he was posted overseas), and Ower Farm afterwards. For many years, Baring's farm manager and general factotum was a forthright character called George Wadey and woe betide any gypsy who thought he would like to park his caravan on Stephen's Castle Down!

Warden Chilcott had developed Woodcote Farm into a stud and Ower Farm into a training stable while Stephen's Castle Down became the gallops. At Woodcote Stud Farm he stood the stallion Black Gauntlet (John O'Gaunt - Usaa), for a few seasons in the late 1930s, having procured the horse from Cheveley Park Stud, Newmarket, and at Ower Farm he installed Harry Lowe as his private trainer. In the old days his

Months of Misery Moments of Bliss

horses had been trained by Frank Hartigan at Weyhill, also in Hampshire.

His best performer was a useful staying 'chaser named Dunhill Castle. By that great sire of jumpers Cottage, he competed in three consecutive Grand Nationals from 1938 to 1940. In latter years Warden Chilcott bred his own horses and they included his last two winners, Cupid's Dart and Flash Colours, at Chepstow in October 1938, both trained by Harry Lowe. Flash Colours had been purchased 'in utero' at the dispersal sale of the late Washington Singer's bloodstock at the 1934 Newmarket December Sales. Flying Colours, the dam of Flash Colours, was one of two mares purchased on that occasion by Warden Chilcott in foal to Lightning Artist, a horse whom Washington Singer stood at King Edward's Place. The other was Liloan (Hurry On - Ixia), who was destined to make her own contribution to this particular story.

In the years leading up to the Second World War, Warden Chilcott ran into financial difficulties and he died at Ower Farm in March 1942. Two months later, Messrs Richard, Austin & Wyatt conducted a private sale of his bloodstock at Salterns where eight lots realised a paltry 1,280 guineas. Half the consignment was purchased by Gerald Deane, the senior partner in bloodstock auctioneers Tattersalls and owner of Littleton Stud on the other side of Winchester. Two of the remaining animals were purchased by the Contessa di Sant' Elia. Most expensive of them were Columbus for whom Gerald Deane paid 800 guineas and Coloan who cost the Contessa 150 guineas. They were both out of Liloan whose third offspring Southborough, then a four-year-old gelding, sold for 52 guineas. Coloan and Southborough then joined Harry Lowe who continued to supervise the yard at Ower Farm.

Meanwhile in 1938 Bill Wightman had a valuable addition to his small string at Dean Farm in the four-year-old gelding Great Barton (Apelle - Praline). Animal lovers worldwide owe his owner, Jockey Club member Major Durham Matthews, a debt of gratitude as he made a gift of his Newmarket house

Getting started as a Trainer

Lanwades Hall to the Animal Health Trust. Great Barton had been gelded prior to arriving from Newmarket where he had savaged Michael Beary on the Heath. Great Barton won his first two starts of the season for his new trainer ridden by the actor Teddy Underdown, who was a very proficient amateur. He then took a step up in class to land the Great St. Wilfrid Handicap at Ripon which in those days was run over a mile-and-a-half. Ridden by the northern professional Harry Blackshaw, he scored by a short head at 100-7 to provide Bill with his first major victory. "At Ripon we were invited as guests of the owner to an hotel near Harrogate to stay the night," he recalls. "We even dressed for dinner. It was simply a different world." Back home things were not on quite such a grand scale as he lived for eighteen months in the Fox and Hounds at Crawley which was run by a couple called Mr and Mrs Friar. "They were lovely people. She was a Scottish lady and a beautiful cook and eventually they moved in to look after Evelyn Baring at Dean Farm."

Another winner to be dispatched from Dean was the nine-year-old gelding Burman (Manna - Lady Burghley). He raced for Sunny Peace's owner Mr G.H. Rumsey, who was a great man for working and show dogs from Wolvershill in Somerset. "We bought this very tall gelding from Charlie Waugh at the Newmarket sales the previous year," Bill says. "I was very young and inexperienced at the time and I asked him if I could borrow the horse's rug to take him home. I remember I got a ticking-off from Charlie for not returning it - I never did it again!"

On July 9, 1939, Bill celebrated his 25th birthday and war was declared on September 3. Little did he realise when giving his great friend Bill Rickaby a leg up into the saddle on Autumn at Salisbury in August that this would be the last runner he would saddle for seven long years - seven years that were to change his life in a way that mercifully no one could possibly have foreseen.

3

A Japanese Prisoner of War

Bill Wightman is a private person. Never one to seek publicity he regards himself as a bit of a loner. While he is happy to talk about all the many horses, good, bad and indifferent that have passed through his hands, not to mention all the colourful personalities with whom he has been associated, he could never be accused of boring anyone with his wartime memories. Although it is well known that he spent three-and-a-half-years as a prisoner of war of the Japanese, he has never disclosed the full horrors of internment. However, he does make the sort of analogy that only a trainer could. "At least I reckon to know exactly how a horse must feel after being given a very hard race."

"War broke out on a Sunday and I joined the 'Newmarket Army' three days later." he explains. "It was all down to my friend Bill Rickaby. He used to ride for me and we went skiing together in Switzerland. I wanted to volunteer for the Army but you couldn't - you were told to go back and wait until you were called up. But Bill Rickaby told me that Major Vernon Spencer Daniel, who was agent to the future Lord Milford at Dalham Hall, outside Newmarket, was bringing a territorial unit up to strength and that if I got there by Wednesday I was in - George Colling, Geoffrey Barling and Bernard van Cutsem were all there.

A Japanese Prisoner of War

"So I joined the Royal Artillery Anti-Aircraft, which was part of the ADGB (Air Defence of Great Britain), stationed at Mildenhall, a base for Wellington bombers. We had some wild nights in Newmarket. One press man called Bob Rodrigo drove straight down the Limekilns which needless to say was sacrilege. Then one day our troop leader, a Captain Lacey-Scott, asked if we had read the London Gazette. 'You've all been gazetted,' he announced. 'Made up into 2nd Lieutenants - take a fortnight's leave and get your uniforms'.

"Geoffrey Barling was my troop commander at Newmarket and during the very wet winter of 1939 we found ourselves under canvas at Corby in Northamptonshire. Bob and Tom Waugh were in my tent and we suffered a certain amount of discomfort despite the pheasants that arrived from Newmarket and the occasional hamper from Fortnums. One day I told 2nd Lieutenant Barling that I had bought a portable wooden shed and asked his permission to erect it on the gun site in place of the bell-tent. We were moved within four days! Incidentally, I think bombardier van Cutsem must be the only man who ever managed to get a double bed into a bell-tent!"

On being posted to RAF Watton in Norfolk, Bill bumped into Geoffrey Barling again. Bill remembers taking Geoff's tunic by mistake in the officers' mess one night - there were just a few khaki tunics amongst all the blue RAF ones and it transpired that they shared the same tailor. Shortly afterwards Bill joined a similar unit in Scotland and while at Kilwinning in Ayrshire, George Colling, who always seemed to wear dress uniform instead of battle dress, put in a brief appearance. So too did Rudolf Hess when he landed just up the road!

"I then moved on to the Orkneys," Bill continues, "and on the Island of Flotta we were visted by some top brass. The brigade major with them happened to be Major V.S. Daniels, who put his hand on my shoulder and said 'you are coming to Brigade Headquarters.' So there was 2nd Lieutenant Wightman, as intelligence officer to the 59th Brigade. It was all done under the old pal's act. But after eleven months I tired of

Months of Misery Moments of Bliss

the job as a staff officer and volunteered to go overseas. Thanks to my brigade commander, Brigadier Cecil Peck, a very brief interview followed in Guildford with Lt-Colonel Sir Ranulph Twisleton-Wykeham-Fiennes, father of the explorer. 'What do you do?' 'I'm a racehorse trainer.' 'You'll do'."

This led to Bill Wightman joining a mobile unit on embarkation leave at Middlesborough. No sooner had the troopship set sail for the Middle East than Pearl Harbour was bombed whereupon they were re-routed to Durban. There they embarked on the Narkunda, an old P & O boat, for the Far East. "Approaching Keppel Harbour in Singapore we were informed that this could be an opposed landing, which was slightly disconcerting as all our equipment was on another ship. There were fighter aircraft scrapping overhead as we disembarked. My troop was supposed to be billeted in the Harbour Board Club, but much to our disgust we got turfed out by the Italian manager and finished up in a local school. We took over manning some anti aircraft-guns and all the while Singapore was being bombed daily. Then out of the blue we were ordered to board the steamship Ipoh and set sail for Sumatra, missing the fall of Singapore by a matter of days."

In Sumatra he saw action at the Battle of Palembang - Palembang was a secret aerodrome. But the allies were over-run and they were ordered to withdraw and proceed as best they could to the port of Osthaven. They then sailed across the Sunda Straits to continue fighting in Java where they were equipped with bren carriers instead of guns. "But we were ordered to lay down our arms and surrender. It was in Java that I had my first experience as a prisoner behind barbed wire. I spent six months in the coolie lines at Tandjung Priok. This was on the docks where we unloaded bombs. We were reasonably well fed but it was the first time that I saw a cut off hand nailed to a tree."

It was as one of a draft of prisoners of war that Bill boarded a tramp steamer, 'destination unknown', only to find himself back in Singapore again. This time he spent a matter of weeks

A Japanese Prisoner of War

in Changi Jail where he was reunited with a number of his old regiment - amongst them a young subaltern who, as James Clavell, was to make his name as a best selling author. For the final three years of the war he was interned at Kuching Camp at Sarawak in Borneo. "At first we spent our time levelling a hill to extend an aerodrome runway. All we had was a 'chunkle', which is like a long hoe, and a basket. But after a while the officers and men were segregated into separate camps. If you made it under the perimeter wire you were likely to get your head cut off but you couldn't escape anyway because the jungle was so dense.

"Whatever the policy of the Japanese Imperial Army was they were having difficulty in feeding us, not that it bothered them much. They would say, 'we can't feed you here so we will move you to somewhere better' and a lot of chaps died on the way. We used to call them the Death Marches. All we had to wear was a G-string and wooden clompers on our feet which we made ourselves. We lived on second rate 'weevily' rice, our rations amounted to about a pint of cooked rice a day, a teaspoonful of sugar, a few vegetables and just enough pork to flavour it. Dysentry, fever and worms were rampant and there were all sorts of different forms of malaria. Most of us had a knife and fork, a spoon and a billy can, but everything in the cook house was made by our own troops. Even the ovens were made from clay out of the ground - they gave us nothing to make them with. And as time progressed so the rations got worse."

Somehow prisoners of war have an amazing capacity for improvisation and their ingenuity defies description. Bill recalls that on the voyage from Tandjung Priok to Singapore they sent a message back to the other members of their regiment by carrier pigeon to dispel rumours that they were the lucky ones being repatriated. "One of our chaps was a bird fancier. He used to trap the wild pigeons in the grain store and one of them was smuggled aboard ship." At Sarawak they even managed to make not only a radio but also a generator to produce

Months of Misery Moments of Bliss

electricity, all from bits and pieces purloined from here, there and everywhere - the flywheel for the generator was made from lead stolen from a tea chest! It was on this home-made radio that Bill Wightman heard that the atom had been split.

Bill never doubted that he would survive. "Human animals are most extraordinarily tough and resilient. There are two outstanding things about life - one is procreation and the other is survival. It's built in. I had one tremendous asset because I had no dependants, no encumbrances if you like. Men with wives and children did nothing but worry and there were more deaths as each successive Christmas passed. At the finish we were burying fifteen men a week, a friend every day. The atom bomb was the only thing that saved us - that's for sure. If they had not dropped the bomb, thousands more British prisoners would have died."

Starved and emaciated, Bill was released in the summer of 1945, whereupon he sailed on an Australian sloop for hospitalisation on the island of Labuan. Here he managed to get himself transferred to a luxurious convalescent home with twelve beds which resembled a Hollywood film set rather than a field hospital. The remaining occupants were all Aussies so Bill made a particular impression when Lady Mountbatten visited the patients. "She sat on the end of my bed for about half an hour and asked me what I wanted. Naturally I said that we would all like to go home as soon as possible and within three days a 'repat' ship came in and picked us up. Unbelievably I had been on the same ship twice before when she was called the Ranchi - first as a P & O steamship when I sailed on her pre-war to Gibraltar and then in the Maldive Islands as an armed cruiser."

By the time this six-footer eventually reached England on November 24, 1945, he weighed only 7st 12lb. Although he was in and out of hospital for an appreciable time, he made a truly miraculous recovery and within a year had saddled his first post-war winner. "I was one of the lucky ones," he says. "I came back and was able to do what I most wanted thanks to the support of Evelyn Baring and my other owners who stood by me, although I had been reported missing for eighteen months."

Although Bill does not consider himself much of a reunion man, he attended a service in Dorchester Abbey in Oxfordshire in July 1993, when the Union Jack from Kuching Camp in Sarawak was blessed and now hangs. "It was the only flag we'd got so it had to be used at all funerals. At first we were forced to bury our dead without coffins, but we scrounged enough timber to make one coffin which we used over and over again. It had a bottom and two sides and on top it was draped with this Union Jack. There were only four of us at Dorchester but a lot of memories."

4

Back in Harness

During the War the few horses that remained in training at Dean Farm had been cared for by Harry Lowe, formerly Sir Warden Chilcott's private trainer at Ower Farm. Although there was very little jump racing in England during that period, Harry Lowe had won a couple of 2 mile 'chases at Windsor in 1945 with Southborough, who raced for Evelyn Baring. That year the Gainsborough gelding put up two other good performances on the Thames-side track finishing second to Lord Bicester's Silver Fame and Lord Stalbridge's Red April, conceding weight to those two high class 'chasers on both occasions.

"After the war I was able to resume training more or less where I had left off," remembers Bill. By then all the horses were stabled at Ower Farm, although he himself continued to live at Dean Farm in the valley. Fortunately there was a loyal staff to rally round although they were missing the original head lad John Every, who had come from South Wonston but had died during the War. However, there was an excellent replacement in Bill Nash, who had served his time with Percy Carter at Chantilly. The stable retained two jockeys; Desmond Dartnall, who had been an apprentice with Wightman back in the pre-war pony days, rode the jumpers and Bill Anderson, who had ridden for a number of years in France where he was attached to Marcel Boussac's stable, was stable jockey on the flat.

Back in Harness

Originally acquired at Warden Chilcott's dispersal sale, eight-year-old Southborough (Gainsborough - Liloan), headed the handful of horses which Bill took over in 1946. "He was a cosy old horse standing seventeen hands. He was very laid back but had a string-halt and had been hobdayed." A grand type of 'chaser, he provided his trainer with a first winner since getting back into harness when scoring in the Westbury Steeplechase over 2 miles at Wincanton in November partnered by Desmond Dartnall - Southborough won the same race again the ensuing season.

By this time Evelyn Baring had sold Southborough to the Contessa di Sant' Elia who was set to enjoy such a fruitful association with Bill Wightman's stable. Married to an Italian count, who was officially an enemy alien during the War, the Contessa had at one time held the courtesy title of Dame of Sardinia to Queen Elena of Italy. But the fact of the matter is the Contessa was a Liverpool lass, given to expressing herself in a typically forthright, north country manner.

The Contessa, a close friend of Sir Warden and Lady Chilcott, used to live in the timber and flint house overlooking the picturesque yard at Ower Farm which has been Bill's home for so long. In latter years Rosamond, who died in 1965 as the widow of the Conte Luigi Arborio Mella di Sant' Elia, rarely ventured from her London home in Grosvenor Square, Mayfair. In racing circles her name is synonymous with Halloween, probably the most popular three-mile 'chaser of the 1950s. Subsequently the Contessa had horses in training with both Peter Cazalet and Ryan Price. The best she had in training at Fairlawne in Kent (an establishment now owned by Prince Khalid Abdullah), was the Imperial Cup winner Antiar. She also bought the Ryan Price trained champion hurdler Fare Time, but he failed to cut much ice in her colours.

Southborough won his share of 'chases in the Contessa's 'cerise, white hoop, armlets and cap', which he carried in successive Grand Nationals. Unfortunately he came to grief on both occasions, in 1949 ridden by Paddy Murray (father of the

Months of Misery Moments of Bliss

late top class flat jockey Tony Murray), behind the 66-1 outsider Russian Hero, and in 1950 when he and Eddie Reavey were never a threat to the great Liverpool specialist, Freebooter. "We really fancied him the first time," says Bill, "as he had shown an aptitude to jump Liverpool when third in the Grand Sefton the previous November. He was going really well in the 'National when he and Lord Bicester's Roimond went for the same gap at the Canal Turn second time round and he came to grief." Roimond finished runner-up to Russian Hero, but only six of the forty-three runners completed the course.

In the spring of 1948 Bill went for a bit of a coup in the Lincolnshire Handicap, the first leg of the Spring Double, which was still run on the Carholme at Lincoln in those days as opposed to Doncaster. And this time he was hoping for better luck than in 1939 when he had saddled the gelded Tap Dancer to finish eighth of thirty-eight runners, a record sized field since the Lincolnshire was first run back in 1853. The horse in question was Evelyn Baring's homebred Final Score.

At two years Final Score (Fair Trial - Arsenal) had been saddled by Harry Lowe to score twice over 5 furlongs at Salisbury. However, he then developed a knee problem and had been off the course for over a year when Bill gave the son of Fair Trial a couple of outings as a four-year-old in November 1947. In the second of them he finished third in a field of thirty-one at Manchester ("in absolutely bottomless ground") and it seemed to his trainer that he had every chance in the following year's Lincolnshire with just 6st 11lb. With the horse giving every satisfaction in his preparation, Mickey Greening was booked to ride and the owner backed him to win a fortune at 66-1.

"Unfortunately the clerk of the weather beat us," Bill says. "Final Score had to have some cut in the ground and it came up firm at Lincoln, so we pulled him out and instead ran him at Hurst Park a fortnight later. Evelyn Baring was abroad at the time but a friend, who had backed the horse and watched the race with me, couldn't see through his race-glasses as his hands

Back in Harness

were shaking so much. I said, 'don't worry, he's a mile in front.' And that's where he stayed although they were catching him towards the finish."

For the first part of that season the top French sprinter Clarion III was based in England and it was only by a neck that he was defeated for the July Cup conceding the winner more than weight-for-age. Ralph Strassburger's colt also finished second in the Lincolnshire, third in the Wokingham Stakes and fifth in the Stewards' Cup, all races earmarked for Final Score. The fact that Final Score defeated Clarion at Royal Ascot endorses Bill's opinion that Final Score could have been top class had he been easier to train. Despite infertility, Clarion made his mark at stud as the sire of Klairon.

Bill actually saddled Final Score on two occasions at that year's Royal Meeting. On the Wednesday he had made most of the running for the Royal Hunt Cup partnered by Bill Anderson and then on the Friday he was one of thirty-two runners in the annual cavalry charge for the Wokingham Stakes - with Charlie Elliot riding, he was only defeated a neck conceding the winner 10lb. Charlie Elliot rode him in his three remaining starts, all over 6 furlongs, winning at Salisbury with consummate ease and the Nottingham Stewards' Cup where he prevailed by a short head. In the interim he had started favourite for the Stewards' Cup at Goodwood behind Dramatic, another son of Fair Trial. That season Bill trained the winners of nine races on the flat, eight of them for Evelyn Baring and one with Kandy Boy for the Contessa di Sant' Elia. The versatile Kandy Boy was homebred out of Southborough's half-sister Coloan.

It had been at the Doncaster September Yearling Sales that one of Evelyn Baring's friends David Shaw Kennedy had acquired Final Score's dam Arsenal (Achtoi - Germinal) from her breeder Major Victor Parr of Ballyboy Stud in Ireland and this was where Final Score went to pursue his career as a stallion in 1950. Trained by Peter Thrale, Arsenal had scored at Newmarket as a three-year-old on Cesarewitch day, having finished runner-up in the Irish Oaks. For the duration of the

Months of Misery Moments of Bliss

War in which he served as an 'elderly' ensign in the Scots' Guards, David Shaw Kennedy leased Arsenal to Evelyn Baring, but as soon as he returned home the mare reverted to Kennedy's ownership.

David Shaw Kennedy always regarded himself as a 'small' owner, but he enjoyed conspicuous success with a number of very cheap yearling purchases trained by Peter Thrale, a veterinary surgeon who practiced in Croydon, where he first took out a licence to train. He later moved to West Horsley and finally to Epsom. Shaw Kennedy was still in his twenties when Nitsichin won him the Irish Oaks and the Cesarewitch. In common with Arsenal, Nitsichin was bred by Victor Parr and was by the resident Ballyboy stallion Achtoi.

Overall, Shaw Kennedy had a remarkable record in the Irish Classics as he also owned Canteener, winner of the 2000 Guineas, Wickbridge, second in the 1000 Guineas, and Manorite, third in the Derby. Manorite had won the Dewhurst Stakes as a two-year-old and he had another top juvenile in Master Gunner, winner of the New Stakes at Royal Ascot in 1949. A son of Nasrullah, he was the first of Arsenal's foals registered in David Shaw Kennedy's name. Master Gunner, who had very suspect forelegs, failed to train on and was unplaced at the next Royal Meeting in the Jersey Stakes - sadly his owner had died just eight days before.

Arsenal continued to exert a singular influence at Ower Farm. Her son Final Score produced his share of winners for the stable, most of them homebred by Evelyn Baring; her daughter Final Draw became a foundation mare for Bill's small stud; and her grandson Badbury Rings was a multiple jumps' winner for the stable. One of Final Score's winners not owned by Evelyn Baring was Mrs Norah Parr's homebred filly Blueit - Bill Wightman saddled her to win a handicap as a three-year-old at the Newmarket July Meeting by eight lengths no less!

5

Heartbreak on the Gallops

An unpalatable truth when it comes to racing is that accidents and injury always seem to involve the best horses - it is commonly known as 'sod's law'. An animal devoid of any ability will happily go through his or her career without any untoward incidents whereas one with real talent somehow seems to court disaster. Even if they don't actually succumb to some accident or injury they find some other means of failing to fulfil their true potential. They are frequently delicate feeders, who leave the trough at the least provocation, or maybe their temperament gets the better of them.

Of all the hundreds of mornings that Bill Wightman has been up on his beloved downs, one stands out above all others. It was more than forty years ago - on the Monday before Royal Ascot in June 1953 to be precise, but he can remember it as though it was yesterday. It is given to very few small mixed stables to have a fancied runner in the Ascot Gold Cup (which was a much more coveted prize in those days than it is today despite retaining Group 1 status), but that year Ower Farm looked like fielding the favourite for the centrepiece to the Royal Meeting in the shape of the four-year-old Kingsfold.

Kingsfold (Kingsway - War Romance) was homebred by Mrs Lawrence Winsland Smith who lived near Coolham, south of Horsham in West Sussex. The name Kingsfold was taken from

Months of Misery Moments of Bliss

a location north of Horsham. Incidentally this is where Mrs Brenda Howlett Nye lives and from her mare Kingsfold Flash she bred the 1995 Jameson Irish Grand National winner Flashing Steel. A daughter of Felstead, War Romance never raced and numerically speaking she was not a successful broodmare, proving barren in seven of the fourteen years that she was at stud. However, in 1949 she foaled a big bay colt who was destined to prove the best produce of the 2000 Guineas winner Kingsway before his export to the USA.

Bill liked Kingsfold from the moment he entered the yard as a yearling, although he realised from the outset that he was a backward individual who would need plenty of time. In fact he had four introductory races in the second half of his two-year-old career ridden by Bill Anderson and on only his second outing finished runner-up to the useful Longstone over 7 furlongs at Lingfield Park, beaten only three-parts of a length. As in all his juvenile starts he was totally unfancied and started that afternoon at 25-1. His trainer was delighted with his progress and the colt went into winter quarters with high hopes entertained for the future.

As a three-year-old Kingsfold finished in the frame in seven of his nine starts, proving a very smart young stayer in the making who looked to appreciate a galloping track. Two of his three victories that season, in April and October, were at Newbury (from 10f to 13^1/$_2$ furlongs), which is one of the fairest courses in the country, while in the interim he scored on another galloping track, Sandown Park. The most important of these wins came in Newbury's Ormonde Stakes (now Group 3 St. Simon Stakes) in the autumn when Kingsfold and Bill Rickaby easily justified favouritism.

That was due compensation for Kingsfold's preceding run when he had finished runner-up to the great Tulyar in the St. Leger, beaten three lengths starting at 66-1. It was a further four lengths back to the third horse, Marcel Boussac's Alcinus, with the enigmatic Gay Time, who had finished runner-up to Tulyar in the Derby, in fourth place. This was a memorable occasion

Heartbreak on the Gallops

for a small stable and it proved the only time that one of Bill Wightman's runners was ever placed in a Classic - not that he ever trained many horses of sufficient merit to compete at that level. It was certainly bad luck to encounter a horse of Tulyar's calibre. This champion was unbeaten in seven starts that season, during the course of which he bettered the British earnings record which had stood for fifty-seven years.

Back in June Kingsfold had shown his liking for an extended trip when runner-up to the year senior Souepi in the Ascot Gold Vase over 2 miles at the Royal Meeting in a field of twenty-one runners ridden by Frankie Durr. "I think it was the first time that they had let his head loose," says Bill with a rueful smile. Kingsfold's seasonal finale came in the Jockey Club Cup over the Cesarewitch course of two-and-a-quarter miles. Here, he turned the tables on Souepi, when as joint favourites they finished second and third, separated by six lengths behind Blarney Stone, the outsider of the four runners. "Kingsfold was an improving colt," said his trainer, "and in the long term anything he achieved as a three-year-old was a bonus."

Bill was convinced that the son of Kingsway would not only stay the two-and-a-half-miles of the Gold Cup but would also relish the extended distance, and the centrepiece to Royal Ascot became his primary objective as a four-year-old. During the spring the colt had three preparatory races over one-and-a-half-miles. After finishing second to Wilwyn in the John Porter Stakes at Newbury, he gained two victories at Newmarket, in the Chippenham Stakes (beating his old adversary Souepi), and the Burwell Stakes.

The Chippenham Stakes was the race before the 2000 Guineas on what could well have been the greatest day of Bill's life. Two years previously at Tattersalls' September Sales in the old Glasgow Paddocks at Doncaster he had been greatly taken by two yearling colts, consecutive lots, consigned from the famous Kildangan Stud in Ireland. He purchased the first of them by The Bug for 3,600 guineas and was underbidder for the second, a son of Nasrullah, at 3,000 guineas. The former was Amapa, who won races for the Contessa di Sant' Elia, but the latter was Nearula, winner of the 2000 Guineas in question! "That's the luck of the draw," says Bill with a smile, "and if you had seen the two together you would not have given Nearula a second glance. You have to admire the chaps who make it their business to buy yearlings at public auction."

Kingsfold finished unplaced on his next outing behind three specialist mile-and-a-half horses, Zucchero, Wilwyn and Worden II, in what turned out to be a vintage Coronation Cup at the Epsom Derby Meeting - Kingsfold had actually led the field down to Tattenham Corner and was still in front as they swung into the straight. The wayward Zucchero was one of the most brilliant performers of his day when consenting to start from the old fashioned barrier, while Wilwyn and Worden were the first two winners of the Washington DC International at Laurel Park in the USA.

Just ten days later Bill was watching Kingsfold do a routine canter ridden as usual by head lad Bill Nash. "The first lot was working in Indian file up the Valley Gallop and just as Kingsfold passed me I saw him falter. Bill Nash pulled him up in a few strides and jumped off. The horse was so lame he could not move. Somehow we managed to put some improvised splints on him and get him back to the yard in one piece. I sent an SOS to my vet, the famous G.P. Male from Reading, and the owner Mrs Smith and they arrived in the yard almost simultaneously.

"By that stage we could not move the horse so we arranged to have the X-ray machine brought to him. The injured hind leg was bandaged; in fact we did everything we could bar putting the leg in plaster. Meanwhile we were all talking together outside his box which had the top door open when there was the most terrific commotion from within. We rushed over to see what was happening - and there was Kingsfold who had gone to have a stale. Of course with an injured hind leg he found it difficult to balance and it transpired that he had sustained a

Heartbreak on the Gallops

delayed fracture; tragically we had to have him put down there and then.

"Kingsfold was a very big horse and a lovely free mover with an extravagant stride on him. Because of this I thought that his run in the Coronation Cup might have been the root cause of the problem. In those days when they pulled up after the finish at Epsom they had to cross a road and there was only a protective layer of peat over the tarmac - I have always thought that was where the damage was done although there were no visible signs of injury. As soon as he was put down I had the injured leg removed and boiled it down. You could see a crack which extended from the bottom of the cannon bone right the way up to within a few inches of his hock. Of course one cannot be certain what happened and I only saw the residue, but it looked as though my assumption was correct. Needless to say the death of Kingsfold, who was only just coming to his best, was a terrible tragedy for all concerned and I never really had as good a flat horse again."

The Form Book indicates that Kingsfold was a superior stayer to his old rival Souepi who duly won the Ascot Gold Cup. Although he was Bill's only Classic placed runner he did actually train for two ladies whose colours had been carried to victory in the Derby. Mrs M. Glenister won the 1949 2000 Guineas and Derby with Nimbus, who was trained by George Colling, whom Bill Wightman nominates as probably the best trainer of his acquaintance. Mrs G. B. Miller owned Mid-day Sun, winner of the 1937 Derby, in partnership with her mother (Mrs J.A.W. Talbot) and trained by Fred Butters - Mrs Miller was the first woman to have her colours carried to victory in the Blue Riband. Alas, nothing Bill trained for these two owners was of the same calibre as either Nimbus or Mid-day Sun!

6

A new Stable Star

'A good big'un will always beat a good little'un', is a well known racing maxim, but it's not one with which Bill Wightman would necessarily agree. Halloween, the best horse he ever trained, was on the small side. "He actually measured over 16 hands, but it was deceptive as he had very high withers," says his handler. "But he was a small framed horse with a noticeably short back, which probably explained why he could be difficult to sit on. Although he had a good shoulder and was good to follow, he did not have a lot in front of him."

Asked to nominate the one quality which made Halloween so special, Bill says unhesitatingly, "guts, he had the heart of a lion. But he was also a natural jumper and an athlete - if he made a mistake he would put his nose on the ground if he could not find another leg. He was as hard as nails and it required a lot of work to get him fit - he would have a month walking on the roads followed by plenty of long, steady canters. Always ready to do his best he was a sweet horse who was never any trouble in or out of the stable - he used to be turned out here in the summer. He was what I call a trainer's horse - in human terms he was the sort that you would want to make friends with."

Like so many good jumpers, Halloween (Court Nez - My Blue Heaven) had a somewhat obscure background. His sire

A new Stable Star

Court Nez was an HIS (Hunter Improvement Society) stallion. These are stallions which are allotted a premium by the Light Horse Breeding Society to travel a certain designated part of the country, the premiums being allotted annually at the HIS Stallion Show held in Tattersalls' Park Paddocks at Newmarket in the spring. The object of the exercise is to provide breeders with a selection of thoroughbred stallions nationwide standing at a modest fee to produce a wide range of quality riding horses for all disciplines, hunting, eventing, dressage, or point-to-points.

Although neither his sire nor his dam ever won, Halloween had an interesting pedigree. Court Nez was half-brother to a very smart two-year-old filly in Veuve Clicquot (Windsor Castle Stakes, Royal Ascot, Chesterfield Stakes, Newmarket), and his sire Bosworth won the Ascot Gold Cup and was half-brother to Selene, the dam of Hyperion, the greatest sire in the first half of the twentieth century. So in the male line he carried the very best blood of Lord Derby's Stanley House Stud.

His dam, the unraced My Blue Heaven (Tai-Yang - Blue Star II), had been bred and conceived at Manna Morriss' Banstead Manor Stud, Newmarket, which is now owned by Prince Khalid Abdullah. Tai-Yang, who was a very unsound individual, had the most extraordinary racing record as he won on his only two appearances in public, as a three-year-old in the Jockey Club Cup and as a five-year-old. Blue Star II was rated the top juvenile filly of her generation in France when she won the Prix de la Foret and Criterium de Maisons-Laffitte. She was a grand-daughter of Jean Stern's great foundation mare Saperlipopette from whom descend Sicambre and a host of other Classic celebrities.

The first recorded foal of My Blue Heaven, Halloween was bred by a Mr F.E. Woodman. At the time Court Nez was based at Mr A.C. Mumford's Tea Caddy Stud at Hannington in Northamptonshire which suggests that Halloween was probably bred somewhere in the Midlands. But according to Bill, Halloween was reputed to have been bred and raised in the

Months of Misery Moments of Bliss

New Forest and found as a foal when he had strayed on to the other side of a ditch from his dam. Whatever the truth, the first positive sighting was made not that far away at a big hunting stable at Bentworth, near Alton, owned by Gerald Barnes of show-jumping renown.

It is conceivable that had Captain Dick Smalley of the Royal Marines not been on the look out for a suitable point-to-pointer to ride, Halloween would never have seen a racecourse. In 1949 Dick retired from the services whereupon he and his wife Joan bought a cottage and some land at Droxford, near Bishop's Waltham. He became a fruit farmer and for a while he also ran Bill's farm. Before the War in which he served mostly with the Mediterranean Fleet, Dick had ridden successfully in point-to-points. Anxious to renew the involvement he telephoned Gerald Barnes one day in 1948 to enquire whether he had anything suitable as a potential point-to-pointer/hunter 'chaser. The answer came back that he did have a couple of unbroken three-year-olds running out in a water meadow which he had got as payment for a bad debt.

In the circumstances one has to marvel that the son of Court Nez had the right identification papers as this was long before Weatherbys issued passports. But Dick Smalley liked what he saw, particularly his exceptionally good hind leg, and bought the youngster then and there for £90. Fortunately Bill Bundy ran a well regarded livery yard at Bishop's Waltham and this was where the little Court Nez gelding was broken-in, but not before he had been cured of the warts that covered his back and shoulders. Prophetically the breaking in was entrusted to one of Bill Wightman's stable men, Jack O'Connor, who worked as a nagsman in his spare time. Jack, who had been apprenticed to Atty Persse, used to drive the Court Nez gelding in long reins around the village and the pair of them would often stop off at a local public house en route. By now he had been named Halloween in memory of Joan Smalley's half-brother Peter Tinn who had been born on All Hallows Eve and was killed in the War.

A new Stable Star

The following summer Halloween and Jack O'Connor made a few appearances at local shows. By that stage both Jack and Dick had discovered to their cost just how difficult their protege was to sit on. Because of his antics, few of the show judges were keen to ride him in the ring and one remarked that he looked much more of a racehorse than a hunter. Although the gelding showed little inclination to jump when Dick took him out that autumn with the local Hambledon Hunt (of which Squire Osbaldeston was once MFH), he determined to qualify him for the next season's point-to-points.

As a five-year-old Halloween had three runs in point-to-points, all Open Races. On his debut at Tweseldown (Staff College Drag), he ran really well to finish fifth in a big field. Back at Tweseldown for the Garth fixture he jumped impeccably to beat Billy D, owned by Len Coville of Hill House renown, the winner of a multitude of races between the flags. Finally he won at the Cowdray on Easter Monday - despite making a serious mistake three from home in the very testing conditions, he defeated Here's Edward who had won a 3 mile 'chase at Plumpton three weeks earlier by fifteen lengths. He returned to the winner's enclosure with his head covered in mud after depositing his rider somewhat unceremoniously on the way!

That autumn Dick Smalley decided to go hunter 'chasing with Halloween. By then he and his wife had moved from Droxford to Roke Farm above Bishop's Waltham, which was only a mile from the Stephen's Castle Down gallops, so it was logical to send the little hunter to Bill Wightman. "I had a full stable at Ower Farm at the time but mercifully I had a spare box and he joined me in January 1951," says Bill. "I had not seen him running in point-to-points, but I had seen him out hunting and frankly he was not very impressive - I certainly didn't think he was anything special. But Bill Bundy had got him hard and hunting fit and he was soon ready to run."

Within three months Halloween had competed in five hunter 'chases without defeat despite the comparative inexperience of his owner-rider. On his debut under Rules, he scored at Windsor in February from two seasoned hunter 'chasers in Jury Star and Monks Crest. He started at 8-1 that afternoon, but he was a short priced favourite in all of his remaining starts that season. Coming back in distance from three miles to two-and-a-half-miles, he then scored at Sandown Park a fortnight later despite being carried wide after the seventh fence. In March he landed the odds in effortless style at Worcester and Sandown Park - at the Grand Military meeting he was always up with the leaders despite some sketchy jumping. Bill recalls that on one occasion at Sandown, Dick was reprimanded by the starter for hanging around out the back which was quite amusing in view of the fact that Dick later became a starter himself!

Finally that season came the Cheltenham Foxhunters'. In fact Halloween had not been engaged originally but the Thursday of the National Hunt Meeting had to be abandoned due to torrential overnight rain. Consequently the Gold Cup and the Foxhunters' were added to the April fixture. The Foxhunters' was reopened and Halloween was duly entered, enabling him to win on firm going in a heatwave. "I remember Dick Smalley came into the paddock looking a bit apprehensive and enquired whether I had any riding instructions for him. I said, 'Well, I've never given you any so far and you've managed alright, but since you insist, I suggest you challenge coming into the last.' And that's just what he did. I think he was the shortest priced favourite ever to win the Foxhunters'." He was returned at 11-8 in a field of twenty-six runners.

Not surprisingly there were tempting offers for Halloween after he had won his two point-to-points, but inevitably his stunning entree into racing under NH Rules really caught the attention of the jumping fraternity. It just so happened that at that time Bill had a specific order to find a three-mile 'chaser for the Contessa di Sant' Elia and he didn't have to look too far. "The only snag was that Joan Smalley was adamant that Halloween was not for sale as he was considered a member of the family. But we gradually increased the ante." In the end the

A new Stable Star

Smalleys agreed to sell for £8,000 (well over £100,000 today), with the stipulation that the horse must stay with Bill Wightman.

However, the transition from hunter 'chasing to open competition was not a happy one. Put in at the deep end, Bill saddled Halloween in the Grand Sefton Trial Handicap 'Chase at Hurst Park in October 1951, ridden by Dick Francis, a leading professional who is now world famous as a writer of best selling thrillers. At that time Dick was stable jockey to the powerful Peter Cazalet establishment at Fairlawne in Kent and with few equals over fences, he was associated with many of the Queen Mother's celebrated jumpers.

On this occasion Dick's partnership with Halloween lasted for only about a mile as the ex hunter fell at the fifth following some indifferent jumping. The race was won by James V. Rank's good horse Greenogue, who made all the running with 12st 3lb, conceding Halloween 2st. Halloween's next attempt in November was even less inspiring. Partnered by stable jockey Desmond Dartnall, he ran in a two-and-a-half mile 'chase at Newbury, but capitulated after meeting the first fence all wrong. "I was watching the race with Monty Smyth, " says Bill, "and after a while he turned to me and said, 'he doesn't need a jockey, he'll win anyway'. And sure enough, he lay up with the leaders all the way, challenged over the last and 'won' going away."

As a result of these two lapses Halloween was reunited with Dick Smalley and to prove that the son of Court Nez had lost neither his form nor his confidence they got back on the winning trail in a couple of amateur 'chases over two-and-a-half miles at Newbury. The second occasion was on a Friday when Bill also saddled old Southborough, who was partnered by Major (later Lt-Colonel) Robin Hastings; he was to become chairman and managing director of the British Bloodstock Agency. The next day at Newbury, Dick Smalley broke his collar bone in a fall at the third fence in a hunter 'chase and consequently plans to run Halloween in the Kim Muir 'Chase for amateurs at the National Hunt Meeting were abandoned.

Instead Halloween was diverted to the Grand National Trial Handicap 'Chase over 4 miles 1 furlong at Hurst Park, where he was allotted 10st 9lb, a weight considerably below Dick's minimum. "I chose Fred Winter to ride him as I wanted someone who could do 10st," Bill recalls. Installed favourite in a field of ten top staying 'chasers Halloween came home eight lengths clear of Devon Cottage and Whispering Steel - beaten out of sight was Cromwell while the 1949 Grand National hero Russian Hero was brought down. It was the beginning of one of the most successful partnerships in the history of National Hunt racing. As Bill points out, "just as there are horses for courses, so there are jockeys for horses."

Prior to Hurst Park, Fred Winter had taken the precaution of asking Dick Smalley what, if anything, was the secret to Halloween only to be told that it was best to give him a free hand and not to sit up his neck - during his formative years he had become accustomed to measuring fences on his own, taking off as he pleased rather than at the instigation of his rider. Dick and Fred were very different in stature as the ex marine is a tall man while the ex paratrooper is quite the opposite - in fact the champion jockey often said that he was far too short in the leg to ride effectively round Liverpool - although that did not stop him riding two Grand National winners in Sundew and Kilmore. Anxious to secure Fred Winter's services for Halloween on a regular basis Bill arranged for him to receive a retainer of £250. "Ryan Price was absolutely furious, but we were good friends. I assured him it would not really affect him as most of his were hurdlers anyway!"

In his prime Halloween proved virtually invincible over three miles on a park course just so long as he had the assistance of Fred Winter. The partnership won nine of the seventeen races in which they teamed up, including the first four starts of the 1952-53 season. They began by winning the Hurst Park Grand

A new Stable Star

Sefton Trial by ten lengths carrying 11st 11lb from Galloway Braes, to whom he was conceding 2lb.

Lady Orde's Galloway Braes became Halloween's greatest adversary. An inveterate front-runner prone to the occasional jumping error, he was one of few top class 'chasers who could match strides with Halloween on a park course - indeed he established a record time of 5m 47s for a 3 mile 'chase in the UK in 1953 when gaining the first of his two victories in the Queen Elizabeth 'Chase, Hurst Park. Galloway Braes was trained by Alex Kilpatrick at Collingbourne Ducis, an establishment which is now utilised by East Everleigh trainer Richard Hannon, having been run as Herridge Stud Farm in the interim by Alex's sons Jim and Sandy. His regular pilot was Bert Morrow, who subsequently joined the staff at Whitsbury Manor Stud, near Fordingbridge.

Halloween and Galloway Braes renewed rivalry in the King George VI 'Chase on Boxing Day. In the interim Halloween had made a winning appearance over course and distance in the Cottage Rake 'Chase, albeit his jumping was hardly in keeping with his starting price of 15-8 on. But there were no such problems in the 'King George' for which Halloween started 7-4 favourite in a small but select field comprising Mont Tremblant, Knock Hard, Stormhead, Galloway Braes and Wenceslaus. In fact it was three of his principal adversaries who made mistakes on this occasion. Coming to the final fence Halloween was challenged by Mont Tremblant. Winner of the previous season's Cheltenham Gold Cup, Mont Tremblant made errors at the last two fences but was still in contention. However, Halloween always relished a struggle and he gradually got the upper hand on the flat to score by a length. Knock Hard, who had trailed the field for a long way after a mistake at the first fence, finished third.

Racegoers at Windsor had a rare treat in January 1953 when Sir Ken landed odds of 10-1 on prior to gaining the intermediate of his three Champion Hurdle victories and Halloween gained his fourth win from as many starts that season in the Herne the Hunter 'Chase as 8-13 favourite. Having won the Champion Hurdle on Sir Ken, Tim Molony partnered Knock Hard in the Gold Cup for which Halloween was installed favourite at 5-2. The race was run in very foggy conditions but as they raced downhill towards the penultimate fence it seemed that both horses were well out of contention. But as soon as they met the rising ground the whole complexity of the race changed. Knock Hard went on to become Vincent O'Brien's fourth Gold Cup winner, beating Halloween by five lengths with Galloway Braes a further two lengths away in third place.

1950/51 (5-6 yrs) Ran 5

Feb 3	WON	Foxhunters' Trial 'Chase, Windsor, by 3 lengths	3 miles	Capt. R. Smalley	8-1
Feb 16	WON	Wilfred Johnstone Hunter 'Chase, Sandown Park, by 5 lengths	2½ miles	Capt. R. Smalley	5-4F
Mar 5	WON	Worcester Hunters' 'Chase, Worcester, by 6 lengths	3 miles	Capt. R. Smalley	8-11F
Mar 16	WON	Past & Present Hunters' 'Chase, Sandown Park, by 8 lengths	3 miles	Capt. R. Smalley	10-11F
Apr 25	WON	Foxhunters' Challenge Cup, Cheltenham, by 3 lengths	4 miles	Capt. R. Smalley	11-8F

1951/52 (6-7 yrs) Ran 5

Oct 24	fell 5th	Grand Sefton Trial Handicap 'Chase, Hurst Park	3 miles	R. Francis	13-2
Nov 29	fell 1st	November Handicap 'Chase, Newbury	2½ miles	D. Dartnall	6-1
Dec 29	WON	Weyhill Handicap 'Chase (Amateurs), Newbury, by 2 lengths	2½ miles	Capt. R. Smalley	5-1
Feb 22	WON	Harwell Handicap 'Chase (Amateurs), Newbury, by 6 lengths	2½ miles	Capt. R. Smalley	5-2F
Mar 8	WON	Grand National Trial Handicap 'Chase, Hurst Park, by 8 lengths	4 miles 1f	F. Winter	7-2F

1952/53 (7-8 yrs) Ran 5

Oct 22	WON	Grand Sefton Trial Handicap 'Chase, Hurst Park by 10l	3 miles	F. Winter	11-2
Nov 29	WON	Cottage Rake Handicap 'Chase, Kempton Park by 5 lengths	3 miles	F. Winter	8-15F

A new Stable Star

Dec 26	WON	King George VI 'Chase, Kempton Park, by 1 length	3 miles	F. Winter	7-4F
Jan 31	WON	Herne the Hunter Handicap 'Chase, Windsor by ³/4 length	3 miles	F. Winter	8-13F
Mar 5	2nd	Cheltenham Gold Cup, Cheltenham	3¹/4 miles	F. Winter	5-2F

7

The Renewal of a great Partnership

One of the most significant events of the 1953-54 season took place at the first fence of the first race on the first day of the new season at Newton Abbot, when the Ryan Price trained entire Cent Francs fell breaking Fred Winter's leg; only the previous season he had been champion jockey with a record 121 winners. Consequently Fred Winter was hors de combat for the duration of the season and Bill Wightman was obliged to find other partners for his stable star. That season Halloween had eight races but only managed to score once. He was ridden by four different jockeys, all top class, but none of them had the same rapport with the little ex hunter as Fred Winter.

The Fred Winter - Halloween partnership is part of National Hunt folklore but ironically Fred Winter had not, in the first instance, been Bill's number one selection. "I cast around for a top jockey who was light not someone who was 11st." he explains. "And I went across to a race meeting in Ireland one day and propositioned Martin Molony in the weighing room about riding Halloween. However, we never got round to talking about money as he said that he had too many commitments in Ireland so I had to look elsewhere."

It was Martin Molony's elder brother Tim who replaced Fred as Halloween's regular partner. The champion National Hunt jockey had previously ridden a winner for the stable on Evelyn

The Renewal of a great Partnership

Baring's five-year-old entire Devonic (Devonian - Leaves of Memory). This was in a novices' hurdle at Cheltenham in October 1951 despite making a couple of serious mistakes. "Tim Molony came into the paddock looking decidedly under the weather and in the course of conversation it transpired that he had got married the previous afternoon!" Not long afterwards Devonic, who was a useful performer on the flat, was sold to Lord Leigh.

The new partnership got off on the right leg when justifying odds laid on over 2 miles in a little race worth just £136 to the winner at Wincanton in November 1953. On his seasonal reappearence Halloween scored by five lengths from the triple Gold Cup hero Cottage Rake, a 14-year-old. But the new combination was then defeated on three consecutive occasions in top class 3 mile 'chases - when second in the Emblem 'Chase, Manchester (to Stormhead), fourth in the King George VI 'Chase (to Galloway Braes, Mont Tremblant and Mariner's Log), and third in the Grand International Handicap 'Chase, Sandown Park (to Mont Tremblant and Domata).

Not surprisingly Tim Molony preferred to renew his association with the preceding year's Gold Cup winner Knock Hard at Cheltenham in March. In the event Knock Hard started second favourite to the 1952 hero Mont Tremblant with Halloween, who had ostensibly lost his form, an outsider at 100-6 ridden by the northern based George Slack, who rode regularly for Bobby Renton's stable. But with the going heavy in marked contrast to the fast ground of the previous year, Halloween did best of that trio, eventually finishing third to two more rank outsiders in Four Ten and Mariner's Log. Reunited with Tim Molony, Halloween was then defeated by Gay Donald in a three horse race at Lingfield Park despite starting at odds on.

On his final two starts that season Halloween finished a good fourth with top-weight of 12st in the Welsh Grand National ridden by Michael Scudamore (father of Peter), and runner-up in the Queen Elizabeth 'Chase, Hurst Park. Worth only

Months of Misery Moments of Bliss

marginally less than the Gold Cup, the Queen Elizabeth 'Chase was run in June on the Monday following the Derby. This novel grand finale to the jumping season attracted a star studded field. Ridden by Jack Dowdeswell, one of the most courageous of all jump jockeys, Halloween started at 100-7, but that did not prevent him finishing runner-up to Galloway Braes, beaten five lengths, with Mariner's Log ten lengths away third in a top class field.

The 1954-55 season was marred by prolonged periods of bad weather which caused the cancelling of meetings up and down the country. It also saw the return of the indomitable Fred Winter to the saddle. At Cheltenham in November 1954 he and the Contessa di Sant' Elia's grand little horse stood once again in the winner's enclosure after conceding Lord Sefton's useful 'chaser Irish Lizard no less than 1st 7lb. "I was schooling him for you all last season," Tim Molony quipped to Fred Winter afterwards. Many a true word is spoken in jest and Bill says that Halloween had actually improved his jumping technique as a result of Tim's style of riding.

The Fred Winter - Halloween combination was resumed at Sandown Park in December where they readily accounted for Mariner's Log and Statecraft in the Ewell 'Chase. Eleven days later on Boxing Day, Halloween attempted to win his second King George VI 'Chase, but the big question was, could he reverse the form with Galloway Braes to whom he had finished only fourth the previous year? Once again Galloway Braes, who was now set to concede his rival 7lb (they had met on level terms the year before), was installed favourite. After two miles the pair of them drew clear of the field, jumping in unison, but Halloween had gained the upper hand by the time they came to the last fence, going on to score by six lengths.

The rivalry between Halloween and Galloway Braes continued on their remaining three outings that season. Back at Kempton Park for the Coventry Handicap 'Chase, the weights were now Galloway Braes 12st 7lb and Halloween 12st 6lb, but the result was the same albeit the winning margin was reduced

The Renewal of a great Partnership

to one-and-a-half-lengths. And so to Cheltenham for the Gold Cup for which Halloween was installed second favourite to the previous year's winner Four Ten. However, the weather nearly put paid to racing altogether. Snow caused the cancellation of Tuesday's card and with a heavy frost over Wednesday night the decision to race on Thursday was not taken until after midday - as a precautionary measure Bill had stopped off en route in Cricklade to buy three or four pounds of butter to spread in Halloween's hooves.

Not only did Halloween get the better of Galloway Braes at Cheltenham but he also managed to defeat Four Ten. But that was still not good enough to secure that elusive Gold Cup victory as Gay Donald scored by ten lengths at 33-1, the longest priced winner in the race's history. Four Ten finished a distant third with the 1953 Grand National winner Early Mist and Galloway Braes the next to finish. Finally that season Halloween started favourite for the Queen Elizabeth 'Chase, Hurst Park, but lost what chance he had by cannoning into the stricken Galloway Braes when the latter fell at the fifth fence.

Next season Halloween made his fourth consecutive appearance in the Gold Cup for which he started at 100-8. Only six days before Cheltenham he had finished third in a handicap 'chase over two-and-a-half miles at Newbury - in the preceding race the stable's highly regarded novice 'chaser Fire Prince had met with a fatal accident. Always a clean limbed horse with legs of steel, Halloween had suffered a rare interruption to his training schedule which had restricted him to only two previous outings that season in both of which he finished runner-up to Galloway Braes' stable companion Pointsman, owned by Sir Percy Orde. Having sustained a leg injury when beaten a short head at Kempton in November, he was off the course for two months until January when going under by two lengths at Sandown Park. In the circumstances it was a brilliant effort by the Contessa di Sant' Elia's 'chaser to finish third in the Gold Cup to the favourite Limber Hill.

Months of Misery Moments of Bliss

Somehow neither Galloway Braes nor Halloween managed to run up to their best form at Prestbury Park. Whereas there was always a doubt about Lady Orde's spectacular 'chaser getting three miles on such a testing course, there were no such worries concerning Halloween - after all he had won the Foxhunters' over four miles. According to Bill the problem was the undulating nature of Cheltenham and the gelding's inability to free wheel downhill. "He always seemed to be left a bit flat footed as they came down the hill when they really turned on the tap and although he always made up a lot of ground afterwards he was always left with just too much to do."

Nowadays there is a dearth of top class 3 mile 'chasers but Halloween was one of a vintage collection that graced the winter game during the 1950s. Amongst those he defeated in four consecutive Gold Cups were such celebrities as Bramble Tudor, Crudwell, Early Mist, E.S.B., Four Ten, Galloway Braes, Glorious Twelfth, Knock Hard, Lanveoc Poulmic, Lochroe, Mariner's Log, Mont Tremblant, Pointsman, Rose Park, Shaef, Statecraft, Stormhead and Teal. They were certainly a star studded collection and must be as distinguished a group of staying 'chasers as any seen during the last forty years.

In view of the fact that Halloween was proven over four miles, it is perhaps surprising that he never ran in the 'National. After all most winners of the Cheltenham Foxhunters' automatically try their luck in the Liverpool equivalent for which Halloween would have been the obvious favourite. However, Bill recalls that there was never any intention of running either in the Liverpool Foxhunters' or the 'National for that matter as it was felt that it would be unfair to ask such a small horse to tackle those formidable Aintree obstacles. "He was a marvellous jumper who never touched a twig," he says, "but we would never have forgiven ourselves had he been injured."

Inevitably Halloween's fortunes were on the decline as an eleven-year-old when he was defeated on his first two starts of

The Renewal of a great Partnership

the 1956-57 season as an odds-on favourite at both Fontwell Park and Windsor. Ridden by Tim Molony, they were his final appearances in public. By that stage Halloween had won seventeen of his thirty-six races under National Hunt Rules and in the process had covered over one hundred miles at racing pace. He was only unplaced on three occasions - the Form Book says he fell twice, but 'unseated rider' would be a more accurate interpretation. All in all it is a record of consistency which has seldom been equalled at the top level and he must be the best 3 mile 'chaser never to win the Gold Cup.

Ask Bill what his abiding memory is of Halloween and he refers not to one of his glory days but to an altogether sadder occasion. "I was walking past his box one morning (the top doors of my boxes were always open), when I heard a noise that sounded just like a pigeon cooing. I went in and put my head to his chest and the noise was the blood pumping through his heart. Of course that was the end of him as a racehorse although his condition stablised in time. In due course the Contessa sent him and Southborough off together to a retirement home near Lingfield where Halloween died some years later from an attack of colic."

Halloween is commemorated every year at Newbury's mid-week fixture in the first half of November by the Hallowe'en Novices' 'Chase over two-and-a-half-miles with £5,000 added and whenever possible Bill likes to make the presentation - the trophy is one of the cups that Halloween earned for the Contessa di Sant' Elia by winning the King George VI 'Chase in the 1950s.

The conditions for the Hallowe'en Novices' 'Chase are as follows: for five-year-olds plus which, at the start of the current season, have not won a 'chase, other than a maximum of two maiden or novice hunters' 'chases, or hunters' 'chases confined to horses eligible to run in point-to-points only, during the two preceding seasons. Weights: 11st each; Penalties: a winner of a 'chase prior to the start of the current season, 4lb; a winner of a 'chase after the start of the current season, 5lb; of such a 'chase value £4,500, 9lb. Allowances: mares, 5lb.

Months of Misery Moments of Bliss

1953/54 (8-9 yrs) Ran 8

Nov 5	WON	Newquay 'Chase, Wincanton, by 5 lengths	2 miles	T. Molony	2-5F
Nov 14	2nd	Emblem 'Chase, Manchester	3 miles	T. Molony	3-1
Dec 26	4th	King George VI 'Chase, Kempton Park	3 miles	T. Molony	7-2
Feb 13	3rd	Grand International Handicap 'Chase, Sandown Park	3 miles	T. Molony	6-1
Mar 4	3rd	Cheltenham Gold Cup, Cheltenham	3^1/$_4$ miles	G. Slack	100-6
Mar 17	2nd	Sussex Stakes 'Chase, Lingfield Park	3 miles	T. Molony	4-5F
Apr 20	4th	Welsh Grand National, Chepstow	3^3/$_4$ miles	M. Scudamore	11-2
June 7	2nd	Queen Elizabeth 'Chase, Hurst Park	3 miles	J. Dowdeswell	100-7

1954/55 (9-10 yrs) Ran 7

Oct 20	2nd	Grand Sefton Trial Handicap 'Chase, Hurst Park	3 miles	F. Winter	11-4F
Nov 11	WON	Charlton Park Handicap 'Chase, Cheltenham, by 1 length	3 miles	F. Winter	9-4F
Dec 16	WON	Ewell 'Chase, Sandown Park, by 3 lengths	3 miles	F. Winter	5-4F
Dec 27	WON	King George VI 'Chase, Kempton Park, by 6 lengths	3 miles	F. Winter	9-2
Feb 26	WON	Coventry Handicap 'Chase, Kempton Park, by 1^1/$_2$ lengths	3 miles	F. Winter	11-10F
Mar 10	2nd	Cheltenham Gold Cup, Cheltenham	3^1/$_4$ miles	F. Winter	7-2
May 30	unpl	Queen Elizabeth 'Chase, Hurst Park	3 miles	F. Winter	5-1F

1955/56 (10-11 yrs) Ran 4

Nov 24	2nd	Cottage Rake Handicap 'Chase, Kempton Park	3 miles	F. Winter	2-5F
Jan 20	2nd	Stanley 'Chase, Sandown Park	3 miles	F. Winter	6-4
Mar 2	3rd	Paddington Handicap 'Chase, Newbury	2^1/$_2$ miles	F. Winter	9-2
Mar 8	3rd	Cheltenham Gold Cup, Cheltenham	3^1/$_4$ miles	F. Winter	100-8

1956/57 (11-12 yrs) Ran 2

| Nov 8 | 2nd | Bury 'Chase, Fontwell Park | 2^1/$_4$ miles | T. Molony | 2-9F |
| Nov 30 | 3rd | Brocas 'Chase, Windsor | 3 miles | T. Molony | 4-5F |

8

Other prominent Jumpers

Trying to find a replacement for a horse of Halloween's calibre is an unenviable task and inevitably brings disappointment, however substantial the available funds and however thorough the search may be. Through the grapevine Bill Wightman heard that Tom Taaffe, who trained at Rathcoole in Co. Dublin and was a regular purveyor of high class jumpers to trainers in England, had an exceptionally nice seven-year-old in his yard named Prince Mildred (River Prince - Lady Mildred).

Prince Mildred had been bred in Ireland at Rathmoyle Stud, Co. Offaly, by Francis O'Toole who also stood River Prince, a noted sire of jumpers. At the time that Bill bought the River Prince gelding on behalf of the Contessa di Sant' Elia, Tom Taaffe was basking in the reflected glory of the 1955 Grand National which had been won by Quare Times ridden by his son Pat, with Carey's Cottage, whom he also trained, in third place ridden by his younger son Tos. Also in the yard at that time was Mr What whom Tom Taaffe would saddle to win the 1958 Grand National.

Such honour and glory were not in store for Prince Mildred notwithstanding his big price tag. "He was a top of the ground horse but unfortunately he proved rather 'duck hearted'," says his handler, "and being a hard puller, who was very difficult to settle, he never really got three miles." During the 1957-58

Months of Misery Moments of Bliss

season Prince Mildred did win 'chases at Newbury (dead-heat) and Hurst Park, when he got every assistance from Michael Scudamore, but it was soon evident that he was never going to be in the same league as Halloween.

Bill can count the number of runners he has had overseas on the fingers of one hand, but Prince Mildred did return to Ireland to compete in the 1959 Galway Plate and during that time he lodged with his former handler Tom Taaffe. Disappointing on that occasion, the best he could manage subsequently was a couple of wins on the tight figure-of-eight course at Fontwell Park. In the first of these he was ridden by John Lawrence (now Lord Oaksey), who performed some commendable acrobatics to keep the partnership intact after a serious mistake at the last fence, an incident which makes Bill chuckle to this day!

In sharp contrast to Prince Mildred his stable companion Oscar Wilde (Epigram - Quenington) had no problems staying three miles, in fact the further they went the better he went. By the same sire as Kingsfold's old rival Souepi, Oscar Wilde was leased with an option to purchase by Thomas Theophilus Jasper, a Southampton solicitor, from Garry Delahooke, who had bought Adstock Manor Stud from Florence Prior. However, the horse had not been bred there, Garry Delahooke having paid just 50 guineas for him as a three-year-old at Newmarket, despite the fact that he had won two races that season over one mile five furlongs.

From the spring of 1958 to the autumn of 1959 Oscar Wilde won four long-distance 'chases for Tom Jasper. That tally opened on a high note with the Welsh Grand National, thus providing stable jockey Brian Lawrence with the biggest success of his career. Runner-up at Chepstow was the Welsh National hero Crudwell who was to retire as the winner of fifty races under both Rules. Oscar Wilde also provided Bill with the opportunity of putting the wind up Garry Delahooke. "Oscar Wilde was ante-post favourite for a big race at Sandown and a day or two before I phoned him and said, purely as a joke, that

Other prominent Jumpers

the owner had asked me to exercise the option to purchase for £800. His reply is unprintable!"

Bill saddled both Oscar Wilde, ridden by Taffy Jenkins, and Royal Tournament partnered by Bert Morrow in the 1959 Grand National. The owner was keen to run Oscar Wilde in the 'National, but the trainer had his reservations. "Unlike Southborough, who jumped Aintree very well - Paddy Murray said he jumped them as if they were hurdles - Oscar Wilde jumped very big and tended to pitch on landing which I thought would be his undoing over those big drop fences." Sure enough Oscar Wilde fell at the fourth fence but Royal Tournament, carrying the colours of Lt-Colonel Martin Gilliat, got as far as the first fence on the second circuit where he refused.

Martin Gilliat, who died in 1993, was the Queen Mother's long serving private secretary, a post he took up in 1956, the year that Her Majesty's Devon Loch collapsed on the run-in to the 'National within sight of victory. Although not a big gambler by any stretch of the imagination, Martin Gilliat was a determined favourite backer and he just could not believe it when Bill told him one day at Cheltenham that Royal Tournament had an outside chance . "Royal Tournament won at 20-1. I think I had a fiver each-way on the Tote - anyway I got a cheque for over £800!" Previously Martin Gilliat's colours had been carried by that old stable favourite Kandy Boy, ridden to victory on one occasion by one of his joint owners Robin Hastings.

One of Bill's neighbours is John Leavett-Shenley who farms at The Holt, Upham. Like another distinguished soldier rider associated with Ower Farm, Major David Gibson, Leavett-Shenley had served in the Welsh Guards and this qualified him to ride his own mare Minimax (Sandyman - Fire Alarm) in the 1953 Grand Military Hunters' 'Chase, Sandown Park, which they won. At about that time he also had a very promising young 'chaser in Fire Prince (Limekiln - Indian Princess), who was registered in Miss Prior's *Half-Bred Stud Book*. He carried the distinctive white colours, with a red, white and blue sash, to four 'chasing victories, ridden in three of them by his enthusiastic owner. Two of those wins had been at Newbury on which course Fire Prince tragically fell at the sixteenth fence when lying second in the 3 mile Jack O'Newbury 'Chase in March 1956, breaking his back. Needless to say his connections were devastated and Bill has always been of the opinion that Fire Prince had what it takes to go to the top. "However, I had made the mistake of winning a novice 'chase with him at Sandown in April, which meant that he started the next season running in handicaps." John Leavett-Shenley followed Dick Smalley in becoming a starter.

The front running Badbury Rings (Blunderbuss - Mons Meg) was one of Bill's most prolific jump winners, although he only took charge of him as a nine-year-old. By the time he was rising fourteen, he had saddled him to win ten 'chases - six of them were at Fontwell Park and six times he was ridden to victory by Owen McNally. On three consecutive occasions Peter Hedger also won on him - he used to work at Ower Farm and now combines training near Chichester with running a horse transport business. Bill recalls putting him up in a 'chase at Fontwell one day. "Looking on tenterhooks, the jockey said, 'I've never ridden a winner over fences,' to which I replied, 'well now's your chance'. And he won!" Badbury Rings was named by his previous owner, Stewart Tory, who used to be one of the country's foremost breeders of Hampshire Down sheep. A great farming family from around Blandford in Dorset, the Torys have long been synonymous with the Portman Hunt and the excellent point-to-point course at Badbury Rings is on their land.

During his time at Ower Farm, Badbury Rings was owned in partnership by Mrs Patsy Tufnell, who lived at nearby Curdridge Grange, and her son Wynne. But for a bad fall he would probably have ridden the old stager in the Grand National, although on his first ride under Rules he put up 29lb overweight! Wynne, who was Bill's assistant for four years, used to run a convalescent home for horses before going to

Other prominent Jumpers

farm at Binstead, near Alton. His sister Meriel has the distinction of being the first lady to ride a winner under Jockey Club Rules, a feat she accomplished at Kempton Park in May 1972. Bill's only other official assistant was Richard Craddock; he subsequently set up a successful bloodstock advertising agency from his home at Wisborough Green in West Sussex.

The pedigree of a horse like Badbury Rings is only of academic interest but it makes fascinating reading in the present context. In 1954, the year that Badbury Rings was foaled, his sire Blunderbuss was responsible for the Cheltenham Gold Cup winner Four Ten, to whom Halloween finished third. Mons Meg, the dam of Badbury Rings, was bred by David Shaw Kennedy out of Final Score's dam Arsenal after the mare had reverted to his ownership from that of Evelyn Baring. Another of Arsenal's daughters, Cherie Marie, became the grandam of a top 'chaser in Easby Abbey (Massey-Ferguson Gold Cup). Two more jumping stars descending from Arsenal's dam Germinal are Titus Oates and Cavvie's Clown.

Ironically, two of the best hurdlers that Bill ever trained were closely related to Classic winners. Anthony Wayne (Windsor Slipper - Bonnie Brae), who was bred by the American, Robert Sterling Clark, was a grandson of his mare Galaday II, the third dam of Never Say Die (Derby, St. Leger). Hilarion (Hyperion - Laitron), whose breeder Sir Percy Loraine was a partner in Kildangan Stud, Co. Kildare (now owned by Sheikh Mohammed), was a half-brother to Dairymaid, the dam of Abermaid (1000 Guineas). Both horses scored six victories over hurdles for the Upham stable - while Anthony Wayne went particularly well for John Maguire, Hilarion did likewise for Michael Scudamore.

Anthony Wayne, who was a top staying hurdler, gained his most important success in the 1955 Christmas Hurdle, Kempton Park. He was owned by John Edney and his daughter and for an interim period was trained under permit from their Hampshire home, The Gables, Houndean. Anthony Wayne had cost only 130 guineas as a four-year-old out of Michael Collins'

Conyngham Lodge Stables on the Curragh despite the fact that he had scored twice that season and been regarded of sufficient merit to run in the Irish Derby. But he had 'a leg' and had been fired and hobdayed. "Anthony Wayne was a nice compact little horse but he made a noise like a chain saw," says Bill. "One day he took off with my travelling head lad Don de Silva up the Valley Gallop and you could hear him a mile away. Mind you he wouldn't normally pull the skin off a rice pudding! But it didn't stop him winning the next day."

Hilarion gained his most important success in the 1956 Berkshire Hurdle, Newbury, for the Contessa di Sant' Elia. A tricky customer, who resented the whip - all the lads had explicit instructions never to hit him - the son of Hyperion always had to be held up for a late run. Subsequently he reverted to the ownership of Mrs J.M. Stephenson who had originally placed him with Harry Gordon-Bowsher at Stockbridge. This lady, who lived at The Old Vicarage, Shiplake, in Oxfordshire, had bought Hilarion as a three-year-old for 3,500 guineas out of Noel Murless's Beckhampton stable. Carrying the colours of his breeder he had won three races that season partnered by Gordon Richards.

"Hilarion was a sweet old horse, a big liver chesnut, but he was a complete con man and we never put him over fences." says Bill. "When he forgot he was a racehorse he used to walk like a camel with his off-fore and his off-hind going forward at the same time - he lacked co-ordination in some way. He was never happy as part of the string. When he had finished working he liked to stand riveted to one spot. Then he would bellow like a lion and come trotting after us. I remember he got a star fracture on the face after a fall at Wincanton one day and the racecourse vet said, 'Your vet can see to that when you get home', which was pretty typical."

9
Two Lady Owner-Breeders

For the 1954 season Bill Wightman acquired an important new patron in Florence Prior, a great authority on the *General Stud Book*, who had just moved from Adstock Manor Stud, near Bletchley in Buckinghamshire, down to her new home Drover's Way at Awbridge, near Romsey on the edge of the New Forest, which is about sixteen miles from Upham. From that moment he found himself combining the duties of trainer with those of chauffeur to a grey haired little lady, who was not quite as frail as she may have looked!

Florence Prior had sold Adstock in the spring of 1952 to Oscar Wilde's owner Garry Delahooke. His son James was to develop Prince Khalid Abdullah's Juddmonte Farms into not only one of the most up-to-date studs in the country, but also one of the most successful. The bloodstock world tends to be a case of wheels within wheels and the man from whom James took over was the former Newmarket trainer Humphrey Cottrill, one of Bill's closest friends. In fact Khalid Abdullah's first Classic winner Known Fact had an overnight stay at Ower Farm prior to running at Deauville in August 1980.

Virtually all the homebred winners that Bill trained for Florence Prior owed their origin to one mare Dutch Clover. Back in 1938 when her father Matthew Prior came out of hospital after a long illness, she decided to buy him a new car

Months of Misery Moments of Bliss

and a filly out of training to cheer him up. She got to hear of a suitable winning Tetratema filly called Entreat with Jack Clayton at Newmarket and, as neither she nor her father could get to see her, the vendor sent her down to Adstock on approval. They liked her and in due course she was mated with the Highclere Stud resident Winterhalter (whose dam Perce-Neige had been bred at Adstock), and produced the grey filly Dutch Clover.

Greatly taken by Dutch Clover, Florence Prior decided to keep her to race, but the trainer to whom she was entrusted returned her within the week on the grounds that she had a decidedly unfriendly disposition. Consigned as a yearling to the 1948 Newmarket December Sales she realised 1,300 guineas before joining Rufus Beasley at Malton. Raced from two to four years, Dutch Clover won six races including the Lancashire Oaks. She then came up for sale again at Newmarket and, having failed to reach a 2,000 guineas reserve, Florence Prior could not resist the temptation of buying her back privately. By then Adstock Manor had been sold so she arranged to send Dutch Clover as a permanent boarder to Leslie Denton's Benham Stud, outside Newbury. She was to prove a good friend to Benham Stud and to Bill Wightman.

Dutch Clover had thirteen foals (seven colts and six fillies), and was only barren twice - she was put down at the age of twenty-two with acute arthritis in a knee. Altogether she produced eleven individual winners from 1954 to 1969. Nine were trained by Bill Wightman for their owner-breeder. They comprised the colts Drover's Way (by Honeyway), Runnymede (by Petition), Pasturage (by March Past), and Herbage (by Queen's Hussar), and the fillies Clover Honey (by Honeyway), Rogation Day (by Petition), Mead (by Honeyway), Aberystwyth (by Aberñant), and Singing Valley (by Songedor).

A grey like his dam, Runnymede, who was bred, foaled and reared at Benham Stud, was a specialist sprinter never scoring beyond the minimum distance and with a preference for soft underfoot conditions. He was also extremely tough and during

Two Lady Owner-Breeders

the course of his first two seasons Bill saddled him on no fewer than seventeen occasions, nine of them as a two-year-old when he was allotted 8st 12lb on the Free Handicap. This represents a well above average number of appearances for a juvenile, but his trainer certainly did well to have him ready to run by the beginning of April as that winter there was snow and frost around for three months.

"We had four inches of snow lying on the ground, no more and no less, from Christmas through to the end of March," Bill recalls. "I used to go up on the gallops on my skis with a sack of corn slung over my shoulder to feed the partridges. Fortunately I have a nice, sheltered, rectangular paddock of fourteen acres close by with a slight rise and we used to work Runnymede and the others round there. There was a fair bit of grass underneath and it wasn't dangerous. It was powder snow and as the temperature never got above minus five degrees, I was able to roll the snow without it clinging."

Never out of the first four that season Runnymede gained three victories at Newbury, the Beckhampton Stakes in April by ten lengths, the Berkshire Stakes in June by two lengths, and the Highclere Nursery in September with top-weight by three lengths, coming late on all three occasions to overwhelm the opposition in the final furlong. Runner-up in both the Salisbury Stakes, where he received a bump at the start, and Ascot's Granville Stakes, the Petition colt put up his best performance that year in the all aged Nunthorpe Stakes at the York festival meeting in August. Taking on the three top sprinters in the country he was rather outpaced by his elders in the early stages, but ran on to such good effect that he was only beaten a length and half-a-length by Matatina and Secret Step, with Sammy Davis a head away in fourth place.

As his own-sister Rogation Day had already proved a useful miler there seemed every prospect of Runnymede staying that trip. But two attempts over 7 furlongs on his first starts of the new season, in the Kempton 2000 Guineas Trial and the Free Handicap, saw him revert to sprinting. In May he won the

Months of Misery Moments of Bliss

Alington Plate, Sandown Park, over 5 furlongs with a characteristic late run to defeat Ruby Laser impressively by two lengths. Thereafter the grey rather lost his way although he put up some good performances in defeat. On successive outings during August and September, he finished second to Roughlyn at Sandown Park (conceding the winner over 2st), fourth in the Portland Handicap, beaten no more than two lengths, and fifth in the Nunthorpe Stakes to Althrey Don, less than four lengths behind the winner.

There was every reason for hoping that Runnymede would have a much more profitable season as a four-year-old. It certainly opened on a promising note with a two lengths' victory in the Palace House Stakes at Newmarket on 2000 Guineas day. Here he beat Holborn and Polyfoto by two lengths and three lengths which seemed to put him in line for top sprinting honours. But he failed to confirm the form behind Holborn in the Temple Stakes, Sandown Park, and was then unplaced to Goldhill in the King's Stand Stakes.

After Royal Ascot the intention had been to run Runnymede in the King George Stakes, Goodwood. However on the morning of the race he was found in a drowsy condition in his box and Bill's own vet said that he exhibited all the symptoms of having been administered some sort of sedative. The horse was taken to the races but was withdrawn upon examination by the racecourse vet. "He took a sample," says Bill, "whereupon he promptly put it in the boot of his car and forgot all about it over the week-end! So that was that. I have always been convinced that he was 'got at', although there was never any satisfactory explanation as to how it happened."

Runnymede never ran again and returned home to Benham Stud as the winner of five races, partnered in all of them by Duncan Keith who was riding on a regular basis for the stable at that time, for total earnings of just £4,623, which hardly seems very much by present day values even allowing for inflation. He commenced covering in 1966 at a fee of 300 guineas for approved mares and he stood as the joint property

Two Lady Owner-Breeders

of Florence Prior, her nephew, John Prior, one of the leading authorities on deer, and her niece, Mrs Prior-Willeard.

Benham Stud, which forms part of Sir Richard Sutton's Settled Estates, is situated adjacent to the busy A4 (the old London to Bath road), between Newbury and Hungerford. Initially Runnymede stood there alongside Songedor under the management of Leslie Denton. He lived a few miles distant at East Garston where he was a dairy farmer in quite a big way and at one time he owned Rhonehurst, the Upper Lambourn yard now presided over by Oliver Sherwood. He also owned a top three-mile 'chaser in Hart Royal but more relevant to the Bill Wightman story he bred the mare Japhette, who was destined to become the grandam of the Cambridgeshire heroine Flying Nelly. Leslie Denton died in November 1967 when responsibilty for the stud and the stallions passed to his widow Margaret and their son Roger. Later he took over the lease and he still manages the stud where three generations of the Hutt family have been stud grooms.

A number of stallions came and went during Runnymede's long innings at Benham Stud, the most important being champion sire Queen's Hussar who spent his retirement there. Runnymede himself established quite a reputation as a sire of two-year-olds and he actually shared the honours with Manacle as the leading sire in that sphere for races won (twenty) in 1974. The principal contributor was Streak and in due course he joined his sire at Benham Stud before export to Sweden. Another of Runnymede's sons, The Go-Between, stood at Herridge Stud Farm en route to Cyprus. Notable amongst Runnymede's daughters is Canton Silk who bred Brocade (Prix de la Foret, Challenge Stakes), dam of 1994 Breeders' Cup Mile winner Barathea.

Florence Prior gave Runnymede to Roger Denton not long before she died in January 1982 and the old horse survived for another four years until he succumbed to the long, hard winter of 1985-86 - he was put down at Benham Stud on February 27. He was twenty-five years of age and his coat was as white as snow.

Months of Misery Moments of Bliss

As well as standing Runnymede at Benham Stud, Florence Prior established a small nucleus of boarding mares descending from his dam Dutch Clover. One of them, Mead, bred Mr Nice Guy for Roger Denton. Born with a deformed muzzle, he was consigned to the 1975 Newmarket October Yearling Sales where East Hendred trainer Eddie Reavey, the man who had ridden Southborough in the 'National and a great buyer of bargain yearlings, purchased him for just 400 guineas. The following year Mr Nice Guy won the Woodcote Stakes on Derby Day, then the first 6 furlong race of the season for two-year-olds. The year after he gave up training Bill was flattered to be asked by Jocelyn Reavey to judge the best turned out for the Eddie Reavey Auction Stakes at the Salisbury June fixture.

Another filly belonging to Florence Prior was Greensward (Mossborough - Stargrass), whom she procured as a yearling for 1,500 guineas at the Newmarket First October Sales from Bernard van Cutsem. Bill says, "Greensward won a couple of races but was very highly strung. Bill Nash spent a tremendous amount of time and trouble with her and it took weeks of patient handling before she could be ridden away. You couldn't put a brush on her and we could never pick her hind feet out - she was never shod behind. I remember Bill Rickaby hurting himself in a very tender place when she whipped round one day just as I was giving him a leg up in the paddock."

Greensward was sold for 1,000 guineas as a three-year-old at the 1956 Newmarket December Sales to Baron Guy de Rothschild for whom she bred Exbury. He proved the top four-year-old in Europe in 1963 when the unbeaten winner of the Prix de l'Arc de Triomphe, Coronation Cup, Grand Prix de Saint-Cloud and Prix Ganay. Even pedigree experts like Florence Prior can all too easily be proved wrong!

When Geoffrey Barling retired from training at the end of the 1973 season, he recommended that one of his owners, Mrs Cuthbert Fleetwood-Hesketh (now Mrs Robert Kennard), a keen hunting lady in her time, should send her horses to be trained by Bill Wightman - the two trainers had remained

Two Lady Owner-Breeders

friends since their wartime days. Having trained at Newmarket since 1932 (he had succeeded his father, Frank Barling, who died in 1935), he was the last in a long line of local trainers whose reputations were established before the outbreak of the War. He is commemorated every year by the Geoffrey Barling Stakes at the Newmarket Craven Meeting in April.

Helen Fleetwood-Hesketh was a niece of one of Geoffrey Barling's owners Oliver Watney, managing director of the family brewing business. He owned and bred horses at Cornbury Park, Charlbury, in North Oxfordshire (where the 1994 Game Fair was held), which was sold on his death to Lord Rotherwick, a cousin of Bill's long standing patron Major Stanley Cayzer. Meanwhile Helen Fleetwood-Hesketh had inherited her uncle's racing colours - her great grandfather Francis Popham owned Littlecote near Hungerford where he bred Wild Dayrell, one of the most romantic of all Derby winners in the last century.

At the 1971 Newmarket December Sales, Geoffrey Barling bought Helen the mare L'Anguissola (Soderini - Posh), carrying to Tower Walk. His choice was easy to understand as she was one of only two mares catalogued in foal to the best horse he ever trained. Runner-up in the 2000 Guineas, Tower Walk developed into a top class sprinter and he had a successful stud career at Limestone Stud in Lincolnshire after starting off in Ireland. L'Anguissola had scored three times as a juvenile including the Selsey Stakes at the festival meeting in July for which the Bill Wightman trained Douane started favourite, but disappointed as a three-year-old.

From three of her first four foals, L'Anguissola produced a trio of exceptional fillies in Walk By, the foal 'in utero' at the time of purchase, Solar and Smarten Up. It is indicative of their class that Bill regarded all three as sufficiently talented to take their chance in the fillies' end of season championship, the Cheveley Park Stakes - and two of them were placed third in what is always one of the most competitive contests at the top level. "L'Anguissola did really well with her daughters." Bill

Months of Misery Moments of Bliss

says, "but it was a different story with the colts from the family - none of those I trained was much good, although they were by such good horses as Ballymoss, Blakeney and Shirley Heights." Of course since then Cadeaux Genereux has helped to paint a very different picture.

Walk By gained her most important win in the 1975 William Hill Portland Handicap, Doncaster, as a three-year-old when she made much of the running to score by two lengths from King of Troy, with her stable companion Import third of the sixteen runners. In the spring Walk By had finished unplaced in the 1000 Guineas behind Nocturnal Spree, but reverting to sprinting, had then finished runner-up to Lochnager in the Finch Decanter Handicap at Ascot in June with the pair of them well clear of the remainder. Here Walk By was conceding the very talented Lochnager no less than 1st 3lb.

Kept in training as a four-year-old, Walk By was to finish third to Music Boy in the King George Stakes, Goodwood. Although Walk By had won the Portland Handicap for 'cock of the north' Edward Hide, her regular partner was Taffy Thomas, who had been apprenticed to Geoffrey Barling and had struck up a rewarding association with Ower Farm. That season he had won the Spillers' Stewards' Cup on Import and he remained faithful to him at Doncaster where the filly was marginally preferred to the colt in the betting. Bill was a great admirer of Taffy Thomas. "Besides being able to ride at 7st 7lb, he was an excellent judge of pace and knew exactly how a horse should be ridden."

The year after foaling Walk By, L'Anguissola produced the Hotfoot filly Solar. Initially her career followed an identical pattern to her half-sister for as two-year-olds both won the Ilsley Plate, Newbury, in June, and the Stockbridge Stakes, Salisbury, in September, and in between were placed in the St. Catherine's Stakes, Newbury. Solar continued to improve throughout the season in the hands of Geoff Baxter, culminating with a brilliant run in the Cheveley Park Stakes. Equipped with blinkers for the first time she was held up early

Two Lady Owner-Breeders

on, but began to make steady progress from half way and, after having every chance at the distance, was eventually beaten two necks in a driving finish with Pasty and Dame Foolish.

Solar was out of her depth in both the 1000 Guineas (to Flying Water) and the Oaks (to Pawneese), the only time that she tackled one-and-a-half-miles, and, although she finished in the frame on another six occasions, she gained her solitary victory in the well contested Hackwood Stakes, Newbury, over 6 furlongs in July, when she came with a well timed run to beat the useful Wolverlife by three-parts of a length.

It is not surprising that Bill should have found Newbury, his nearest flat course apart from Goodwood, an ideal fixture at which to run his juveniles in the first half of the season. Whereas Walk By and Solar both won the Ilsley Plate in June, their half-sister Smarten Up won on her debut in the Chattis Hill Stakes at the July fixture. Runner-up on her next two outings, at Newbury and Salisbury, she then finished third to Sookera and Fair Salinia in the Cheveley Park Stakes, where she was promoted a place on the disqualification of the second, Petty Purse, to whom she had finished runner-up in the Stockbridge Stakes. The Sharpen Up filly was always amongst the leaders at Newmarket and was one of the principal sufferers when crossed by Petty Purse in the final furlong.

Unlike Walk By and Solar, Smarten Up did not compete for the 1000 Guineas as her run in the Fred Darling Stakes at Newbury confirmed the impression that sprinting was her forte. Next time out she made all the running to win the Temple Stakes, Sandown Park, but was caught on the line by another filly in Oscilight who shared the spoils. Not only are they the only members of their sex ever to win this important Sandown Park sprint in its thirty year history, but it was also the first time that this stiff 5 furlongs had been run in less than 60 seconds. Smarten Up reserved the best performance of her entire career for her finale at York in August - in the William Hill Sprint Championship (which has now reverted to its original title Nunthorpe Stakes), she endeavoured to make all the running

Months of Misery Moments of Bliss

and only succumbed to the odds-on favourite Solinus with the remainder of the field well in arrears.

In 1977 Helen Fleetwood-Hesketh married Major Bobby Kennard who had served in an Indian cavalry regiment and trained horses in India and Australia. The following year they bought Woodminton Farm at Bowerchalke in Wiltshire, which is a few miles out of Salisbury on the Blandford road and had been part of the Pembroke Estate, where they developed a small private stud. Helen Kennard brought L'Anguissola with her from her home at Holcombe Rogus in Devon and she was joined by her three daughters, Walk By, Solar and Smarten Up.

To the end of 1994, Smarten Up produced seven individual winners from eight runners with ten foals of racing age. These are highlighted by champion sprinter Cadeaux Genereux (by Young Generation), who was conceived and foaled at Whitsbury Manor Stud, outside Fordingbridge, which, although across the county boundary into Hampshire, is no distance from Woodminton Farm.

With the purchase of Woodminton Farm, the Kennards took on the mantle of commercial breeders and, instead of putting their colts into training with Bill Wightman, they started selling yearlings at the Newmarket October and Houghton/Highflyer Sales. A 210,000 guineas purchase by Sheikh Maktoum Al Maktoum in 1986, Cadeaux Genereux replaced his own sire Young Generation at Whitsbury Manor Stud where he has proved a very successful young stallion. The racing world was shocked when that horse's erstwhile trainer, Alex Scott (34), was found murdered at his Newmarket home in September 1994. His mother Lady Scott had the occasional horse in training at Ower Farm and Alex used to come over from their home Rotherfield Park near Alton to ride out in the school holidays.

In 1993 Helen and Bobby Kennard sold Woodminton Farm and moved to a bungalow in Lambourn. Situated on Hungerford Hill, it overlooks Peter Walwyn's yard at Windsor House where they have their few horses in training. Mind you

Two Lady Owner-Breeders

Bill used to say that the best owners were those "who lived abroad, and corresponded by cheque!"

10

The M.P. who bought the National Stud

In 1966 Bill Wightman had saddled Isis, owned by Frank 'Butch' Bullen, to finish second in the Cambridgeshire, beaten a head by Dites in a field of thirty-four runners, thus foiling an ante-post gamble from 66-1. The Upham trainer had to wait until the first leg of the Autumn Double in 1974 to avenge that defeat when Simon Wingfield Digby's Flying Nelly, partnered by David Maitland, who ironically had ridden Dites to victory at Newmarket, prevailed by two heads. On this occasion the Irish Sweeps Cambridgeshire had attracted another enormous field with thirty-nine runners, but the four-year-old filly held on with the utmost gameness to resist the challenge of Kew Gardens and Traquair.

Flying Nelly (Nelcius - Flying By), was a grey bred by Robert Sangster's Swettenham Stud, then based at his Cheshire home Swettenham Hall, and sold by him as a foal at the 1970 Newmarket December Sales for 3,500 guineas to the BBA acting on behalf of Simon Wingfield Digby of Sandley Stud in Dorset. A key figure behind the purchase was Christopher Watkins, then manager of Sandley Stud, which was the home of the National Stud before it moved from Gillingham to Newmarket. Chris Watkins, who later managed Woolton House Stud for the Hue-Williams before leasing Wyld Court Stud on the other side of Newbury, now runs Blackmore Vale Stud next

The M.P. who bought the National Stud

door to Sandley Stud. This is currently the home of the stallions King's Signet and Karinga Bay. Coincidentally Chris Watkins had actually foaled Flying Nelly when he was a student with Tim Rogers at Airlie Stud in Ireland and Flying By was visiting one of the stallions there.

"When she was a yearling Simon Wingfield Digby asked me to come over to Sandley and take a look at Flying Nelly," Bill recalls. "She had a slightly enlarged hock and he wanted to know if I thought it was strong enough to stand training." Her record speaks for itself. In training for four seasons, Flying Nelly raced twenty-six times in her owner's apple green and black colours and scored six victories. Invariably held up in her races she was capable of a fine turn of finishing speed. The Cambridgeshire is over the unusual distance of 9 furlongs and she also gained two good wins over the stiff Sandown Park course in the Benson and Hedges Anniversary Handicap (8 furlongs), at four years, and the Centenary Cup (10 furlongs), at five years.

Flying Nelly is the best offspring of the otherwise disappointing French Derby winner Nelcius and she belongs to the second crop of foals that he sired at Meddler Stud, Newmarket, before being dispatched to Japan. Her dam Flying By, who did all her winning over the minimum distance, was placed in such prestige events as the Prix de l'Abbaye de Longchamp, Nunthorpe Stakes, Duke of York Stakes and King George Stakes. As mentioned earlier in connection with Runnymede, Flying Nelly is a grand-daughter of Japhette, who was bred at Benham Stud from Leslie Denton's foundation mare Port Beam, a family synonymous with speed.

Simon Wingfield Digby, whose own family has been indigenous to Dorset since the second half of the 17th century and who was Conservative MP for West Dorset for over thirty years, bought the old National Stud in 1965 having previously bred horses in the grounds of the family home Sherborne Castle. The foundation mare should have been Feria, who was bought as a two-year-old from the executors of Jim Dewar in

Months of Misery Moments of Bliss

1954. Unfortunately it did not work out that way. Winner of the Fred Darling Stakes and third in the 1000 Guineas on her first two starts for her new owner, she was not the first good race filly to prove an abject failure in the paddocks.

It has really been Flying Nelly who has proved the cornerstone of Sandley Stud. She herself is the dam of six winners, amongst them her two daughters Nelly Do Da (by Derring-Do), and Bustling Nelly (by Bustino), both of whom returned to Sandley where they are accredited with six and five winners respectively. Nelly Do Da was trained by Bill Wightman and Bustling Nelly by Barry Hills, who has had such enormous success with Flying Nelly's son Further Flight. In 1994 this grand stayer became the first horse to win four consecutive Group races in the British Isles when winning the Jockey Club Cup. Then in September 1995 the nine-year-old grey gelding won the Jockey Club Cup for a fifth successive time thereby recording his twenty-first victory for owner-breeder, Simon Wingfield Digby - and surely no winner at Newmarket has ever received a bigger ovation.

Back at the 1960 Newmarket September Sales, Bill paid 2,600 guineas on Simon Wingfield Digby's behalf for an Elopement colt bred and conceived at the old National Stud. Named Elan he only managed to win a maiden handicap at Lingfield Park as a three-year-old, whereupon he was consigned to the Newmarket December Sales. He was bought there for just 580 guineas by Bob McCreery, but only afterwards did he realise just why the colt was so cheap - he turned his off-fore out very markedly. Nowadays Bob McCreery, the breeder of High Top and Old Vic, runs a very successful commercial stud at Stowell Hill, near Templecombe, which is just across the county boundary from Sandley into Somerset, but in those days he was known as a leading amateur rider. However, Elan was to make his name for the Epsom trainer John Sutcliffe Snr, winning a division of the Gloucestershire (now Supreme Novices') Hurdle and Schweppes Gold Trophy.

The M.P. who bought the National Stud

Another very successful foal purchase attributed to the BBA for Simon Wingfield Digby was a son of the Royal Hunt Cup winner King's Troop and the unraced Aries, who cost 6,400 guineas at the 1973 December Sales. Named Air Trooper, this colt was bred by, and consigned from, St. Quentin Stud in Sussex owned by Anthony Askew. His brother Gerald had paid 30,000 guineas for Air Trooper's grandam Refreshed, who had finished third in the 1000 Guineas, at the dispersal of Jim Dewar's bloodstock in December 1954. The Askew brothers were nephews of another major player in the bloodstock world James V. Rank. At the same sale, Anthony Askew paid a record 36,000 guineas for Refreshed's half-sister Festoon, winner of that year's 1000 Guineas.

The Lincoln and the Cambridgeshire cater for horses of similar ability so it is not difficult to appreciate the improvement shown by Air Trooper during the course of his four-year-old career. He was balloted out of the first leg of the Spring Double when allotted 7st 4lb - instead he ran in the apprentice handicap, the opening event on the Lincoln card, and finished fourth - but received 9st 7lb in the second leg of the Autumn Double, a challenge he declined. This staggering rise in the weights of over 2st reflected the amazing improvement the King's Troop colt, who was previously regarded as nothing more than a useful handicapper, had achieved within the space of eight months. The racing press attributed that transformation to the adornment of blinkers but his handler says that it was the ground that made all the difference. "People always assume that horses will run faster with blinkers in the same way that the stewards think if you hit a horse it will run faster. Air Trooper had to have top of the ground - I have never known anything make so much difference."

Air Trooper won three competitive handicaps in April, the Rosebery Handicap, Kempton Park (by four lengths), Newbury Spring Cup (by three lengths), and Sandown Cup (by six lengths). Held up on all three occasions he came with a

Months of Misery Moments of Bliss

commendable turn of foot in the closing stages to win convincingly. That sequence ended when he was fourth in the London Gold Cup at Newbury (formerly a feature at the defunct Alexandra Park), and unplaced in the Queen Anne Stakes, Royal Ascot, where he could make no impression over the last two furlongs. Back in handicaps, he then won two good prizes in July, the Hong Kong Handicap, Sandown Park, and the John Smith's Magnet Cup, York, under 9st 6lb.

There was a slight conflict of interests over the Hong Kong Handicap as Bill had intended running his own horse Bell-Tent. "The trouble was they were both top of the ground horses. I felt that this was an ideal race for Bell-Tent and Pat Eddery had already approached me to ride. But Simon Wingfield Digby and his son-in-law Richard Hardy were keen to run and I didn't want to have two runners, so I pulled mine out. As I said to the owner, 'I only run mine for fun, I train yours professionally!' "

Air Trooper only had two further outings in the second half of the season. Anchored with 9st 10lb when third in a handicap at Sandown Park, he reserved the best performance of his entire career for his penultimate outing. At his second attempt in a Group race he seemed outpaced early on in the Queen Elizabeth II Stakes (then Group 2), at Ascot in September, but failed by only a head to peg back, Trusted, another handicapper made good, with the enigmatic Radetzky a length away in third. The unplaced favourite was the northern challenger Don.

The intention had been to keep Air Trooper in training as a five-year-old with the express intention of winning a Group race, but after finishing tailed off in the Westbury Stakes at Sandown Park on his seasonal reappearance, it transpired that he had a wind problem. So it was decided he should be retired forthwith to Sandley Stud for the 1978 season where he replaced Import's sire Porto Bello, who had moved on to pastures new at Herridge Stud Farm. Put to stud late, Air Trooper only covered nine mares that season which yielded just five foals. One of four fillies was Bill Wightman's homebred Cheri Berry of whom more later.

The M.P. who bought the National Stud

Had Air Trooper won the Queen Elizabeth II Stakes instead of finishing a close second it would have made all the difference as by that time breeders had become conditioned to the idea that stallions must be Group winners, the Pattern System having first been introduced in 1971. Consequently Air Trooper was never fashionable and he had made little impact as a stallion by the time he left Sandley Stud for Sweden as a 13-year-old in 1986. Ironically commercial breeders like nothing more than a miler, but nowadays it has to be a winner with the all important black type indicating success in a Group or Listed race.

Just two months after Air Trooper had run so well in the Queen Elizabeth II Stakes, Bill procured his half-brother, a Queen's Hussar foal, as one of the lots belonging to the St. Quentin Stud dispersal at the Newmarket December Sales. He was bought on behalf of a syndicate of his owners for the not inconsiderable sum of 22,000 guineas to resell as a yearling in anticipation of Air Trooper further enhancing his reputation in the interim. Although that part of the plan did not come to fruition the transaction still showed a healthy profit as the colt realised 30,000 guineas when consigned as the property of a syndicate from Sandley Stud at the following year's Houghton Sales.

More recently St. Quentin Stud at Hartfield in Sussex was leased by Mrs Rosemary Newton who, together with her cousin Trevor Mountain, was a patron of Ower Farm. The best winner Rosemary Newton ever owned was probably Silver Birch who helped to provide Bill with two of his best juveniles in latter years. They are her grey son Golden Birch, whose little known sire Heights of Gold stood at St. Quentin Stud, and her grandson Star Hill (Star Appeal - Pook's Hill). He won four races as a juvenile for his owner-breeder Trevor Mountain, including the Bonusprint Sirenia Stakes (Listed), Kempton Park, in September 1989. On all four occasions Star Hill was ridden by John Williams for whom Bill Wightman had a

Months of Misery Moments of Bliss

particularly high regard. "Like Taffy Thomas he never hit a horse hard and they always ate up afterwards."

Also bred by Rosemary Newton was the good looking Divine Pet (Tina's Pet - Davinia), one of Bill's last notable handicappers. Returned after being sold as a yearling at the Newmarket Autumn Sales, he was operated on for his wind at Bristol University and never looked back. On two occasions during the 1990s, he was strongly fancied for the Stewards' Cup - he was balloted out the first time and then had to miss the race the following year due to a minor set-back in training shortly beforehand.

11
More big Handicap Successes

During the 1970s Bill Wightman saddled a succession of top handicap winners, either sprinters or milers, which gave rise to him being labelled a 'handicap specialist' by the racing press. This, as he explains, is something of a misnomer. "The fact of the matter is that this was the class of horse I was training. As they were not good enough to win weight-for-age races, there was no alternative but to place them in handicaps. It was a very different game then as nowadays everyone speaks to the handicapper. We were busy trying to outwit the handicapper - you had to try and get on a handicap mark where you could win."

'If at first you don't succeed, try, try again,' was certainly the policy pursued with Privateer (Pirate King - Pretty Cage). Gelded as a juvenile, he was homebred by Donald Colebrook, who lived at Frobury Farm, Kingsclere, the village on the borders of Hampshire and Berkshire where Ian Balding presides over one of the most historic training establishments in the country. Privateer won the 1972 William Hill Portland Handicap at Doncaster having been third the preceding year and second the year before that. He showed improved form to win as a six-year-old, turning the tables on the previous year's winner Most Secret. That season Privateer had been beaten unluckily in the Stewards' Cup when finishing a head runner-

Months of Misery Moments of Bliss

up to Touch Paper. The race was a great tribute to the handicapper as in a blanket finish less than a length covered the first six home. Altogether Privateer won eight races and was successful in every season from two to six years. In fact he was still in training at Upham as a 10-year-old, proving a most reliable lead horse with the passing of the years, quite apart from being one of the stable's favourites.

Bill has a particularly soft spot for Privateer as he had also trained his dam Pretty Cage but unfortunately he was not blessed with the best of forelegs. "He was very pigeon-toed. The owner wanted to sell him as a yearling but I dissuaded him by saying that nobody would want to buy him with those joints - his legs could have graced a Jacobean table!" Bill had bought Pretty Cage as a yearling at Newmarket for just 300 guineas. Already named, she was consigned from Sir Victor Sassoon's Eve Stud which owed its name to his initials E.V. (Ellice Victor). It was just a coincidence that Pretty Cage, who gained four of her six wins as a juvenile, was by Cagire II, a horse which had been trained at Kingsclere in the days of Evan Williams. Subsequently Donald Colebrook named one of Pretty Cage's offspring Kingsclere and Bill won a couple of small races with him.

It is not easy to keep a four-year-old filly in top form from March through to September but in 1974 Bill saddled Tom Parrington's Somersway (Will Somers - Belle of Victor), to finish runner-up in the Irish Sweeps Lincoln on her seasonal reappearance, while on her finale she won the Burmah Castrol Ayr Gold Cup, two of the most competitive races of the season. In the interim she won handicaps at Kempton Park and Newcastle. The Lincoln and the Ayr Gold Cup always attract large fields and there were twenty-six runners in the former and twenty-three in the latter. In Scotland's richest race lightweight Des Cullen kept Somersway on the best ground up the centre of the course (the going on both sides had been badly cut up over the two preceding days) to foil a gamble on the Irish trained Sarasota Star ridden by Lester Piggott. The filly was thus

Months of Misery Moments of Bliss

Dulwich College cricket XI 1932: W.G.R. Wightman (back row 4th left): S.C. Griffith (front row 2nd left). (*Sydney S.Walbridge*)

Months of Misery Moments of Bliss

Sunny Peace (Desmond Dartnall), who became Bill Wightman's very first winner in 1937.

Cutting a dash pony racing at Northolt Park pre War.

A young gunnery officer in 1940 prior to being posted overseas.

Months of Misery Moments of Bliss

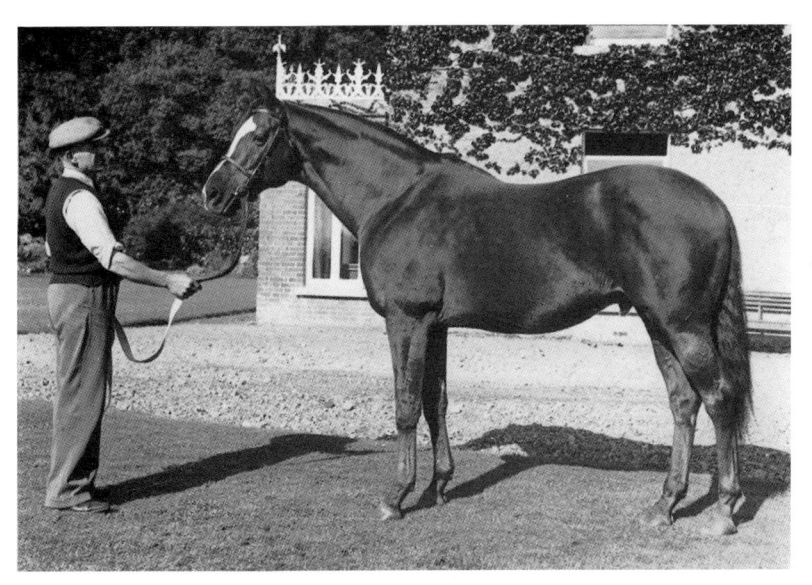

At Ballyboy Stud, Co. Meath: Final Score helped to put his trainer back on the map after his return from a Japanese prisoner of war camp. *(W.W. Rouch)*

Kingsfold, who was probably the best flat horse trained at Ower Farm, broke a leg on the gallops just before the 1953 Ascot Gold Cup. *(W.W. Rouch)*

Months of Misery Moments of Bliss

Bill Wightman and Halloween with travelling head lad Don de Silva (left), and head lad, Bill Nash. *(Evening News & Hampshire Telegraph)*

Months of Misery Moments of Bliss

Halloween with his owner, the Contessa di Sant' Elia *(Thomson Picture Service)*, and with Fred Winter at Kempton Park on Boxing Day 1952 prior to their first victory in the King George VI 'Chase. *(W.W. Rouch)*

Months of Misery Moments of Bliss

The string returns to the picturesque main yard at Ower Farm built of flint and brick. *(William G. Wooldridge)*

Months of Misery Moments of Bliss

Runnymede in retirement at Benham Stud, where he was bred, foaled and reared and spent the duration of his career as a stallion. *(Fiona Vigors)*

Import (M. Thomas), wins the 1975 Spillers' Stewards' Cup at Goodwood - his trainer's local course. *(Press Association)*

Months of Misery Moments of Bliss

Watching the string on Stephen's Castle Down: Bill Wightman on his homebred Bell-Tent with Bill Nash at his head. *(W.W. Rouch)*

It was the guv'nor who had to pay the Bills!: Ower Farm stalwarts, Bill Anderson (left), Bill Nash and Bill Drakeley in retirement. *(Derek Chamberlain)*

More big Handicap Successes

emulating her own-brother Kamundu who won the 1965 Ayr Gold Cup.

The winner of seven races, at two, three, four and five years, Somersway had been purchased as a yearling at the Newmarket Houghton Sales by her trainer for 2,900 guineas in the draft from Victor Stud, Co. Tipperary, on behalf of his neighbours Michael and Susan Pakenham. She is a daughter of Lord Leverhulme, owner-breeder of the Derby runner-up Hot Grove. "When the Pakenhams came to see Somersway as a yearling one of their friends commented that she looked more like a store jumper," says Bill, "so I had to make sure that she won as a two-year-old which she did at Salisbury on the second of her three juvenile starts thanks to Geoff Baxter's expertise and style of riding!"

Somersway represented a well known 'nick' being by Will Somers out of a mare by The Phoenix, two speed horses which used to stand at Ballykisteen Stud. Ballykisteen was affiliated to Victor and they were two of the leading commercial studs of that era in Ireland. Upon her retirement Somersway was boarded at her trainer's Ower Farm Stud. But having failed to get in foal to her 1976 covering by Sharp Edge, who then stood at Littleton Stud, outside Winchester, the mare was exported to Australia the following year. In those days Littleton was owned by Bruce Deane, who succeeded his father, Gerald, as a partner in Tattersalls. In due course Bruce sold the stud to the present owner, Jeff Smith of Lochsong renown, and moved his breeding operation to Bishop's Down Farm, next to Bishop's Waltham.

Not many stallions can claim to have sired a Group 1 winning sprinter and a Grade 1 winner over fences but this has been the singular achievement of Import with Fearless Lad and Young Hustler respectively. Import (Porto Bello - Immortelle) was one of the best sprinters that Bill ever trained and he bought him, not at one of the fashionable yearling sales at Newmarket, but at the Autumn Sales of 1972 when he cost 7,000 guineas from his breeder, Mr J.B. Eastwood. He belonged to the first crop of the sprinter Porto Bello who was then standing at Sandley Stud in Dorset. Many good sprinters come from relatively obscure families but Import has classic distaff relations. His dam Immortelle is an own-sister to Lionhearted, who finished runner-up in the Irish Sweeps Derby, and his grandam Thunder is an own-sister to Lightning, the dam of Parthia and a half-sister to Alcide. These were all stalwarts of Sir Humphrey de Trafford's Newsells Park Stud in Hertfordshire, now owned by Issam Fares.

Although Import was so stoutly bred on the dam's side he proved to be a very resolute sprinter and was approaching top class - like Air Trooper he liked to hear his feet rattle. In the July Cup at Newmarket as a five-year-old he finished third at level weights to Lochnager and Three Legs, beaten only three parts of a length and a neck. Up with the leaders from the start he managed to keep his head in front for a furlong from about halfway - amongst the also rans was the dual Prix de l'Abbaye de Longchamp hero Gentilhombre.

However, Import is best remembered as a sprint handicapper with major victories in the Spillers' Stewards' Cup, Goodwood, at four years, and the Wokingham Stakes, Royal Ascot, at five years, in both of which he was equipped with blinkers and partnered by Taffy Thomas. In fact he ran in three consecutive Stewards' Cups, winning the intermediate of them. An extremely consistent individual, he won seven of his thirty-seven starts and was placed eighteen times. His placings include a second in the Ayr Gold Cup, beaten a short head by Roman Warrior (another son of Porto Bello), and thirds in successive Portland Handicaps at Doncaster, on the second occasion to his stable companion Walk By.

In his first three seasons Import raced for his joint owners Major Stanley Cayzer and the American, Edward B. Benjamin, but the partnership was dissolved when Bill Wightman bought Import back on Stanley Cayzer's behalf for 17,000 guineas at the 1975 Newmarket December Sales in between his Stewards' Cup and Wokingham Stakes triumphs.

More big Handicap Successes

Stanley Cayzer is a member of the shipping family that owned the Union Castle Line which sailed the weekly mail boats between Southampton and South Africa. "It was while I was staying at the Carlton in Johannesburg that I first met my good friend Humphrey Cottrill," relates Bill. 'Hello what are you doing here?' quizzed the Newmarket trainer, 'trying to get away from people like you,' was the quick rejoinder! I had flown out to South Africa but we came home together on board a Union Castle ship. Our wives Lola and Toni sat on the deck sunning themselves all day while Humphrey and I did a fair bit of drinking. We all had a marvellous fortnight!

"Stanley Cayzer, who was master of the Warwickshire Foxhounds, had a lovely grouse moor up in Scotland and I used to get invited for a week's shooting. I was into labradors in quite a big way in those days thanks to Jack Waugh who gave me Stripe in the 1960s. I remember going up there one year in a new Range Rover - it was one of the early ones without any power steering and it was the worst car I ever had! I said to the assembled party, "Don't think I've just come all the way up here for the grouse shooting, I've come to win the Ayr Gold Cup'. And I did with Somersway!" In those days Stanley Cayzer lived near Banbury, but he then moved to the Channel Islands. It was at the close of the 1994-95 season that Douglas Hunt, who had been with the Warwickshire under Stanley Cayzer, retired from hunting hounds with the Hambledon, Bill's local pack.

Like Helen Kennard, Edward B. Benjamin (Stanley Cayzer's partner in Import), had been one of Geoffrey Barling's owners. When on the look out for a suitable successor to Barling, Benjamin remarked, "I don't care if he's a good trainer, just so long as he's honest!" Edward Benjamin, who came from New Orleans and made a fortune from real estate, also owned a stud, Starmount Farm, in North Carolina. The best horse he owned here was probably the 1966 Derby third Black Prince II and he was also the owner-breeder of the Queen Mary Stakes heroine Visp, both trained by Jack Watts. In his native country he was

Months of Misery Moments of Bliss

the breeder of Canonero II and the owner of Nantallah, amongst other top horses.

Import retired to stand at Hunsley House Stud near Beverley in the old East Riding of Yorkshire for the 1977 season. It was after his great run in the July Cup that he was bought by three friends, Bob Urquhart, who had inherited the stud from his grandfather Edmund Vernon Stephenson, Anthony Gillam, a grandson of the great Yorkshire owner-breeder Major Lionel Holliday, and Ripon farmer William Turner. Bob Urquhart, who used to manage Whitsbury Manor Stud for William Hill, is still at Hunsley House, whereas Anthony Gillam acts as a stipendiary steward. A former amateur rider and owner of Copgrove Stud, he once trained Red Rum for Freebooter's owner Mrs Lurline Brotherton.

During his first five seasons at Hunsley House, Import sired some smart flat winners, amongst them Fearless Lad (King's Stand Stakes, Royal Ascot), and such useful handicappers as Wiki Wiki Wheels, Miss Import and Trwyn Cilan, but by the time he had taken up residence at Chesters Stud in Northumberland after interim periods in Berkshire and Bedfordshire he had become regarded as a NH stallion. Import's move to the jumping orientated Chesters Stud adjacent to Hadrian's Wall near Hexham came in the wake of one of his first successful jumping produce Jamesmead. He was bred by Mick Channon out of Cathy Jane whom Bill Wightman saddled to win the Brown Jack Stakes at Ascot. From Chesters, Import moved to his present home, Seamus McAleer's Drum Road Stud, Cookstown, Co. Tyrone, Northern Ireland.

In 1973, 1974 and 1975, Bill saddled three members of the fair sex, Queendom, Somersway and Flying Nelly, to finish runner-up in the Irish Sweeps Lincoln. This unfortunate sequence was finally set to rights when Geoff Baxter drove home King's Ride (Rarity - Ride) in the 1980 William Hill Lincoln to score by a short head from Blue Bridge. He started third favourite in a field of eighteen runners which seemed more of a reflection on his trainer's record than that of the

More big Handicap Successes

horse. The fact was he had taken an inordinate amount of time to win a race, only managing to lose his maiden certificate in November of his three-year-old days when he scored twice within the space of three days. "There is no doubt he had ability," Bill reflects, "but I never thought it would take so long before we won with him or that we would have to campaign him as far afield as Stockton (Teesside Park)."

King's Ride was a useful handicapper but he was none too consistent and had a marked preference for soft or even heavy going. The winner of six races, at three, four and five years, he was also placed on numerous occasions notably when second in the Jockey Club Stakes (beaten decisively by Master Willie), Newbury Summer Cup and Rosebery Handicap, Kempton Park. In 1982 the Rarity horse was sold to stand as a National Hunt sire at Peter and Ann Downes' Russellstown Stud, Co. Westmeath, where his owner David Barry Clark boarded a few mares to support him. Bill describes him as "the most understanding of owners", and on retirement another of David Clark's useful horses, Martinosky, went to join his son-in-law Giles Bravery at Newmarket.

A farmer and seed merchant from Great Totham, near Maldon in Essex, David Clark had paid 22,000 guineas for King's Ride, a half-brother to Court Chad (Hungerford Stakes), at the 1977 Houghton Sales when the third lot in the catalogue. One of the reasons he was of interest to the owners of Russellstown Stud was that he came from the same family as that excellent sire of jumpers Celtic Cone as well as the champion hurdler Lanzarote. A proven National Hunt sire, King's Ride is now one of the stars at Liam Cashman's Rathbarry Stud, Co. Cork.

12

Some old Stalwarts

Buried at Ower Farm is that grand old campaigner Pneumatic (Fun Fair - Spring Lady). The winner of seventeen races, he must be the best bargain that Bill Wightman ever procured. "He was a horse who improved with age, but needed top of the ground." Bill originally bought him on spec. After running initially for his wife Antoinette he raced for most of his career in the Contessa di Sant' Elia's cerise and white colours, which had been made famous by a very different celebrity in Halloween, before reverting back to Toni's ownership. Today one of his trainer's most prized possessions is a portrait of Pneumatic by Juliet MacLeod.

It was at the 1952 Newmarket October Sales that the Upham trainer dashed out into a cloud burst (the old ring in Park Paddocks was a very small, wooden structure, far removed from the present emporium), to buy this yearling colt for 65 guineas from Mrs Renee Robeson's Southcourt Stud, near Leighton Buzzard. At the previous December Sales the son of Fun Fair had been sold in the same ring by his breeder Mr G.E.F. North for 100 guineas. Geoffrey Ford North, who used to train and ride his own horses, had bought one of Bill's earliest winners Petrograd. "I remember walking down Prince's Street in Edinburgh in my battledress during the War and meeting Geoffrey, who was serving in the 10th Hussars,

Some old Stalwarts

looking frightfully smart complete with boots, breeches and spurs."

Ask what attracted him to Pneumatic in the first place Bill replies, "He was made the right way and having trained a half-brother, Dogberry, who had ability but was a jady customer like his sire, I thought this one might turn out alright." Gelded shortly after his arrival at Ower Farm, Pneumatic ran seventy-eight times and was ridden to twelve of his seventeen victories by Doug Smith. He was also placed on another thirty-three occasions. Probably better at 5 than 6 furlongs, he gained the reputation as a Newbury specialist. On the Berkshire course he won his first race as a two-year-old in June 1953 and his last as a ten-year-old in August 1961. In the interim he won Newbury's Round Oak Handicap over 5 furlongs at the October fixture on four occasions - nowadays it is a handicap over 10 furlongs.

Bill thinks he may have duped his old friend and neighbour, the handicapper George Smith who lived at West Meon. "One day he came over to see the horses. Old Pneumatic was turned out in a paddock right beside the house and he was covered in mud. I told George the old gelding was seven or eight and was past it and he dropped him a stone in the handicap!" It gave Bill particular pleasure when he won the inaugural George Smith Memorial at Newbury with Import in June 1974. Old Pneumatic rendered yeoman service in retirement for he was a marvellous 'anchor' for young stock turned out beside him; he was put to sleep at the advanced age of thirty in 1981 and is buried in the garden.

It was close to Newbury that another of Bill's very shrewd purchases Fraxinus (Supreme Court - Ash Tray), was bred by the executors of Thomas Lilley, who together with his wife Vera (later Mrs Roger Hue-Williams), owned Woolton House Stud at Woolton Hill; Tom was at one time chairman of the family footwear business, Saxone, Lilley and Skinner. Following the death of Tom Lilley, Fraxinus came up for sale as a yearling at Newmarket in October 1961. But he failed to make his reserve and Bill was able to buy this member of the Reine Mab family privately. "The stud manager G.F. Luckings was determined that I should buy him. I said, 'I don't have that sort of money' - he said, 'it wasn't very much'. I remember saying that your not very much isn't what I would call not very much! Then to my amazement he said, '£200'. I didn't hestitate and he certainly went on to earn us a bit of silver."

Coincidentally, Fraxinus' own sire, the Woolton House bred Supreme Court, had also been unsold in the ring as a yearling whereupon Tom Lilley made a present of him to his wife. Placed initially with Marcus Marsh at Newmarket the colt had to find alternative accommodation to make way for an influx of the Aga Khan's horses, so Supreme Court was transferred to Evan Williams at Kingsclere and he duly won the inaugural King George VI and Queen Elizabeth (Festival of Britain) Stakes.

Like Pneumatic, Fraxinus started off racing in Toni Wightman's black and green colours. The big pay day came at Goodwood in August 1963 when ridden by David 'Flapper' Yates he took the lead 6 furlongs from home in the News of the World Handicap and ran on well to hold Peter Piper by a neck. At that time the most valuable handicap for three-year-olds over one-and-a-quarter miles, it was staged on the fourth and final day of the then once-a-year meeting on Bill's local course. That afternoon Fraxinus earned his connections a first prize of £8,633, which equates to about £100,000 in present day values. "He had a high knee action and used to bounce off the ground like a golf ball on concrete," says his handler.

Effective on an undulating track, Fraxinus won another good prize as a four-year-old when making all the running to win the Brighton Challenge Cup over one-and-a-half miles. In later life the son of Supreme Court was plagued with leg problems which were remedied in the short term by firing, but he eventually broke down competing in his final race at Lingfield Park as a seven-year-old. That year he was exported by the BBA for stallion duties in New Zealand.

Some old Stalwarts

Equally adept at training jumpers or flat horses, it seems rather incongruous that Bill Wightman had a superior record with sprinters and milers than with middle-distance horses and stayers, at least when it came to the bigger races. Three of his best staying handicappers, Roxburgh, a gelding, Aureate, an entire, and Cathy Jane, a filly, all of whom were fancied Cesarewitch outsiders at some stage of their careers, exemplify his extraordinary versatility in the art of training.

Bill's association with the Rickman family, which owned and bred Roxburgh, dates back to the Final Score era. The Upham trainer remembers Eric Rickman, who was the racing correspondent of the *Daily Mail* from 1929 to 1949 writing under the pseudonym Robin Goodfellow, enquiring whether to back Final Score at Hurst Park after the horse had missed his scheduled reappearence in the previous month's Lincolnshire. "I told him to help himself." says Bill. The horse duly obliged at the very rewarding odds of 100-6. A new friendship was forged and for years the two pitted their wits against one another as members of the Twelve Club where kindred spirits nominate twelve horses to follow during the course of the year.

Eric Rickman had two sons, John, who succeeded him as racing correspondent of the *Daily Mail* and became such a popular figure when racing was launched on ITV, and Geoffrey, a lawyer by profession who bred horses at his Bookham Lodge Stud at Stoke d'Abernon in Surrey. The foundation mare of his small private stud was Brighton Rock - she was bought through the BBA for 270 guineas at the 1954 Newmarket December Sales carrying to Mossborough. The resultant foal was Roxburgh.

"Roxburgh was so slow as a two-year-old that he couldn't get out of his own way," says Bill. "So I asked Brian Swift, whose opinion I valued, to come over and ride him and let me know what he thought with regard to the horse's future. Fortunately he said it was too early to draw any firm conclusions but for which we would almost certainly have sold him on." Invariably equipped with a rubber gag, Roxburgh became a smart stayer

Months of Misery Moments of Bliss

with ten victories on the flat including the Rosebery Memorial Handicap, Epsom, and Midland Cesarewitch, Birmingham; he also holds one record which is in no danger of being beaten - for 2 miles at Hurst Park! Latterly he was owned by Mrs N. Stuart-Cuff for whom he also scored four times over hurdles and was runner-up in the Imperial Cup to Antiar. Ironically Antiar was owned by the Contessa di Sant' Elia and trained for her by Peter Cazalet.

Bill also trained Roxburgh's winning half-brother Commuter (by Faubourg II). Sold as a three-year-old at the Newmarket Autumn Sales for 1,000 guineas to George Forbes of the Veterinary Bloodstock Agency at Epsom, he became something of a celebrity in India where he won three of the most important races in Calcutta, the Calcutta Gold Cup, Governor's Cup and Queen Elizabeth II Cup. Commuter had been consigned to the sales along with eleven-year-old Prince Mildred, the replacement for Halloween, who was acquired by Tim Forster, then training at Letcombe Bassett, outside Wantage.

One of two daughters of Brighton Rock trained at Ower Farm was Roedean with whom her owner was very anxious to win a race as she was by that great broodmare sire Big Game. "I remember telling Eric Rickman that I wanted a medal if I ever won a race with her. After ten unsuccessful attempts, she eventually managed to do so in a weakly contested maiden handicap at Yarmouth. I think all the other jockeys must have been on our side!" The other daughter was the non-winning Charybdis (by Chanteur II). She was to serve Geoffrey Rickman well by breeding Joshua - he proved a top miler trained by Alec Kerr, whose Dorking yard was no distance from the owner's home. In due course Geoffrey Rickman built Blackthorn Stud at Six Mile Bottom on the outskirts of Newmarket specifically to stand Joshua. Later this was sold to Ahmed Foustok who renamed it Cedar Tree Stud.

Aureate (Aureole - Fair Maiden) came to Bill after he had been bought as a four-year-old for 2,700 guineas by the BBA

Some old Stalwarts

out of Cecil Boyd-Rochfort's Freemason Lodge Stables at Newmarket where his sire was also trained. That season he had scored twice over 2 miles at Lingfield Park. A big, good looking horse, Aureate needed strong handling and an extended distance to be seen to advantage. Aureole's offspring were known to be temperamental and by the time Bill Wightman trained Aureate as five-year-old he had his own ideas about racing. In the circumstances he did well to finish second in three good long distance events, the Chester Cup, Brown Jack Stakes and Cesarewitch. Starting at 33-1 at Newmarket, he was beaten a neck by Mintmaster. In 1966 Aureate left for New Zealand, the year before Fraxinus embarked upon the same journey.

Whereas Aureate had actually fallen when attempting to emulate Roxburgh in the Rosebery Memorial at the Epsom Derby Meeting, Cathy Jane went one better than Aureate when winning the 1973 Brown Jack Stakes at Ascot in July. The Brown Jack Stakes, which commemorates one of the most popular racehorses of all time, used to be staged over an extended 2 miles 6 furlongs and, together with the Queen Alexandra Stakes run over the same course and distance, was the longest flat race in Great Britain - it is now run over 2 miles. But for a well orchestrated public campaign to save the Queen Alexandra Stakes in 1994 this marathon would have been axed by the authorities.

Cathy Jane (Lauso - Mrs. Flurry), who had changed hands as a foal and as a yearling at Newmarket for just 360 guineas, was the first racehorse owned by international soccer star turned racehorse trainer Mick Channon, who raced her in partnership with his Southampton FC colleague Brian O'Neill. In due course Cathy Jane, who came to Ower Farm as a backend two-year-old from Ken 'Window' Payne, became the foundation mare of Mick Channon's stud. Bill had a particular liking for her sire, Lauso. Winner of the Italian Derby and sire of the Ascot Gold Cup winner Precipice Wood, Lauso stood at Willie Stephenson's Tudor Stud in Hertfordshire.

Months of Misery Moments of Bliss

Jamesmead Stud Farm at Fair Oak between Southampton and Winchester was about three miles from Ower Farm and Cathy Jane's first foal Man on the Run made that short journey prior to becoming her dam's first winner. In due course the stud produced two notable jumpers who excelled at Newbury. In February 1988 Import's son Jamesmead (after whom the stud was named), won the Tote Gold Trophy and in November 1989 Ghofar won the Hennessy Cognac Gold Cup, both trained by David Elsworth. Jamesmead and Ghofar are of particular interest to Bill as he trained their respective dams Cathy Jane and Royale Final. The latter was bred by owner-trainer-breeder, Herbert Blagrave, president of Southampton F.C. Import ended up standing in Northern Ireland and that was where Jamesmead retired to stud - at Ian Duncan's Lennymore Stud, Crumlin, Co. Antrim.

The Oaks Trial Stakes at Lingfield Park, which has had a string of different sponsors over the years, has diminished in prestige from Group 3 to only Listed status, but there was a time when it was just as important a trial for the Oaks as the equivalent Derby Trial Stakes remains for the Derby. In 1967 Ower Farm provided the winner in Javata (Javelot - Tena Mariata), for Mr J.D. Morgan from Felden, near Hemel Hempstead. However, it proved a bit of a flash in the pan as next time out the filly was beaten as an odds-on favourite for the Lancashire Oaks. Javata was duly exported to the USA never to be heard of again.

That season Bill recorded his one and only success on the Continent. In December he saddled Spunyarn (Narrator - Alpine Dance) to win at Saint-Cloud ridden by champion jockey Yves Saint-Martin. Spunyarn was homebred by Commander and Mrs Toby Marten from Crichel in Dorset and their small stud sprang to prominence in 1989 with their brilliant two-year-old filly Dead Certain, who was another David Elsworth celebrity. Subsequently Spunyarn won in Geoffrey Lowndes' colours - he then farmed at Hambledon but

Some old Stalwarts

subsequently bought Roke Farm at Bishop's Waltham where Dick and Joan Smalley used to live.

Over the years the weights for the Free Handicap show that Bill Wightman trained two exceptional two-year-old fillies although neither Solar nor Metair, who were foaled in consecutive years, won a race of great importance. However, both were rated only 2lb below the top juveniles of their sex. In 1975 Solar was allotted 8st 11lb behind Pasty to whom she had finished third in the William Hill Cheveley Park Stakes and in 1976 Metair was allocated 8st 6lb behind another Cheveley Park winner Durtal.

Metair (Laser Light - Treatisan) did not run in the Cheveley Park as her connections decided to let her take her chance the following afternoon over a furlong less in the competitive Bentinck Nursery carrying joint top-weight of 9st which included a 7lb penalty. Ridden by Taffy Thomas, she showed admirable resolution to score by half a length giving the runner-up 21lb. That was Metair's fourth win from her last five starts and, but for being knocked out of contention by another runner at the start of a nursery at Goodwood, it would have been five out of five. Two other wins had been recorded at Salisbury thereby providing her trainer with a fourth victory in the Stockbridge Stakes (now Dick Poole Stakes), within the space of five years, following Somersway (1972), Walk By (1974), and Solar (1975).

The following season, Metair kept up the good work with three successes. She emulated Solar by winning the Hackwood Stakes (Listed), at Newbury in July and then defied top-weight of 9st 10lb in the Wykeham Handicap at the York festival meeting in August. Shortly afterwards Metair was sold to Humphrey Cottrill (acting for Prince Khalid Abdullah), who had been responsible for the filly going to Bill in the first place; he had originally bought her for his friend Oliver Pike of Metair Freight. Metair became just about the very first mare Khalid Abdullah ever owned before his breeding operation became known as Juddmonte Farms. The price was undisclosed but it would have been many times greater than the 1,600 guineas she had cost as a yearling at the Newmarket October Sales from Rathduff Stud in Ireland where she was bred. "She had what it takes and was one of those rare fillies you could train with your eyes shut."

Not many yearlings make the grade from Ascot Sales to the Derby field, but Goblin (Sun Prince - Rocelle) was just such a case. Bill bought him for 3,600 guineas on the second day of the Ascot Sales (which were held in those days at the old Windsor Forest Stud) in December 1976, when consigned anonymously as 'the property of a gentleman'. Eighteen months later Goblin belied his odds of 200-1 to finish a highly creditable tenth of twenty-five runners in the Derby behind Shirley Heights. Lester Piggott had ridden him to win a two-year-old maiden at Newmarket at the back-end in a big field by three lengths establishing a new course record for the Dewhurst Stakes course. On dismounting, he enquired, "and where have you been hiding this bugger then?"

Just why Goblin should have been consigned to Ascot in the first place is a bit of a mystery. The fact of the matter was he had been bred in Ireland by John Sunley and had been entered at Goffs' Premier September Yearling Sale from Sandville Stud. This stud in Co. Cork was owned by John Magnier and managed by Gay O'Callaghan, the same team involved with Castle Hyde Stud where Sun Prince stood. Castle Hyde was then affiliated to the embryo Coolmore establishment of which John Magnier was a founder director.

A member of Sun Prince's first crop and the first foal of his dam, Goblin was bought by Bill Wightman on behalf of the author and playwright William Douglas-Home, a younger brother of the Conservative Prime Minister, Lord Hume, who lived not far from Upham at Drayton House, East Meon. He is best remembered in racing circles for his play, 'The Jockey Club Stakes', an amusing parody on Portman Square. Bill trained Goblin to win six races, at two, three and four years,

Some old Stalwarts

whereupon he joined William's son Jamie, who had just taken out a licence to train at East Hendred.

No record of Bill's expertise at both buying and training would be complete without reference to one of his last notable performers, Single (Jellaby - Miss Solo). He was sold by Mrs Maggie Hunt, an owner at Ower Farm, at the 1983 Newmarket Autumn Sales for just 300 guineas. Maggie Hunt had bred Single and his dam Miss Solo and both had been conceived at Benham Stud, the former by Jellaby and the latter by Runnymede. Single gained the last of his eleven victories in the Swinley Forest Handicap at Ascot in September 1987 as a five-year-old ridden by Pat Eddery, who had struck up a particular rapport with the old gelding. Single was to enjoy a happy retirement hunting with the Cotswold.

13

Homebred Winners

Just as the human population is more or less equally divided between the sexes, so too is the thoroughbred species. Over a period of sixty years, Bill Wightman must have trained a comparable number of fillies to colts and inevitably some of them have gone on to prove top broodmares. Three that spring readily to mind, who had diverse talents on the racecourse, are Greensward, dam of Exbury, Smarten Up, dam of Cadeaux Genereux, and Flying Nelly, dam of Further Flight.

As a man who has always enjoyed country pursuits, the role of thoroughbred breeder was a natural progression so it is not surprising that Ower Farm should develop a stud as an appendage to the racing stable. A farmer too, Bill was also in the fortunate position of having the necessary land around the yard to develop into paddocks which over the years have proved just as useful for turning out horses in or out of training as for breeding stock, so the two entities have always worked together well. He has also been able to keep stud expenses down to a reasonable level by growing a certain amount of his own fodder and forage as well as boarding mares for clients and owning mares in partnership with various friends.

In terms of breeding Bill is the first to admit that he has always operated at the bargain basement level, never paying big prices for mares or for nominations. His very first mare Final

Homebred Winners

Draw (Foxhunter - Arsenal), a half-sister to Final Score and Master Gunner, was a present from her breeder Evelyn Baring for whom she had proved disappointing both on the racecourse (she split a pastern) and at stud. Barren in four of her first five stud seasons she produced Dompas to a mating with the jumping sire Domaha, the second of her only two foals. Domaha was chosen because he stood at Ardenrun Stud in Sussex owned by Gerry Langford, MRCVS, who had a reputation for getting bad breeders in foal.

Although she was never broken Dompas was to prove her worth as a broodmare. All seven of her offspring scored in one field or another, albeit one Copper Rambler did so over fences, and another Stupa was a point-to-pointer. Bill leased two of her daughters for racing. Zugela (by Zucchero), who became a useful broodmare herself at Ower Farm, won the competitive Crockford Handicap for three-year-olds over 2 miles at Sandown Park for Mrs Gwen Hunt from Littleton outside Winchester, and Modom (by Compensation), scored three times for another lady owner, Mrs Bridget Edwards.

Modom's daughter Balmy Breeze (by Idiot's Delight) is now her owner-breeder's solitary broodmare. In 1995 she was one of the first to be certified in foal to the new Blackmore Vale Stud resident Karinga Bay. Also conceived at Blackmore Vale was Balmy Breeze's half-brother In the Zone (by Martinmas). Owned, trained and bred by Bill, this gelding became his very last winner under National Hunt Rules when scoring in a novices' 'chase at Fontwell Park on the 1993 May Day Bank Holiday. Starting at 20-1 he was ridden by Peter Hobbs. Bill remembers the occasion with mixed feelings. During the course of the race In the Zone cut an artery on his off-fore and the powers that be insisted that he underwent a routine dope test before being allowed to receive treatment to the leg wound from which he lost a lot of blood.

Dompas' three remaining flat winners raced either for Major W.D. Gibson or his wife Charlotte whose home at Greenhill House, was within a mile of Ower Farm, where Bill and Toni lived when they first married. A regular soldier in the Welsh Guards and a shipowner, David Gibson is a great nephew of Lord Glanely, one of the great patrons of the Turf between the two World Wars. David, who became a member of the Jockey Club's National Hunt Committee which at that time had responsibility for jump racing, had made his name as an amateur jockey. In the 1950s he rode the winner of the Grand Military Gold Cup four times, on Klaxton (1950/51/52), and Cottage Lace (1956).

Predictably all three of David and Charlotte Gibsons' Dompas yearlings went into training at Ower Farm. The best of them proved to be Kingdom (by Tudor Jinks), the winner of five races on the flat, who subsequently scored under NH Rules, and Queendom (by Quorum). Queendom proved a very able miler with an excellent turn of foot winning six races, at three and four years. She was also second in two major handicaps in 1973, the Irish Sweeps Lincoln to Bronze Hill and the Trafalgar House Handicap, Ascot, to Blue Cashmere. Had Queendom won the Lincoln she would have provided the Littleton Stud resident Quorum with a remarkable Spring Double as that year his son Red Rum won the first of his three Grand Nationals.

The Gibsons boarded Queendom at Ower Farm Stud where her first foal was Charlotte's Choice (by Blakeney). "He was a bonny little horse," says Bill. "Charlotte Gibson chose to send Queendom to Blakeney, hence the name. It was slightly out of keeping for her to choose a stayer as she liked them to run as two-year-olds. But I did manage to win a nursery with Charlotte's Choice at the back-end although I had to put a pair of blinkers on."

Sold privately to another of Bill's patrons Richard Green, proprietor of the well known sporting gallery in Dover Street, Charlotte's Choice won eight races altogether. Successful in three good handicaps over one-and-a-half miles as a three-year-old, the Kenneth Robertson Handicap, Newbury, Rosebery Memorial, Epsom, and Great Yorkshire Handicap, Doncaster,

Homebred Winners

he was gelded over the winter but soon recovered to gain his most important win in the Ladbroke Chester Cup over 2 miles 2 furlongs on the Roodeye in May. It was slightly fortuitous that Charlotte's Choice ran at Chester as the trainer explains, "His owner Richard Green telephoned to say that he was not keen to run, but as I thought the gelding had an outstanding chance, I told him he had already left for Chester!"

The only filly which Queendom produced for the Gibsons was her second foal, the winning Queen's Niece (by Great Nephew). She has kept the family going and is the grandam of a couple of useful two-year-olds of recent vintage in Gadge and Louis' Queen. It is quite a coincidence that they were both consigned to the sales as yearlings from Sandley Stud which has had such a long association with Ower Farm.

Back in 1955 Bill had won a small race at Worcester with Fabrication for the executors of the late Bill Stratton. He was a sporting farmer who had run in the Powderhall Sprint in Edinburgh as a young man and trained his own horses. Four years later Bill paid 330 guineas at the Newmarket July Sales for Fabrication's two-year-old half-sister, Chilcombe Belle (Robert Barker - Treachery), when submitted by her owner-breeder Luke Bull. At three years the filly carried Bill's own colours to victory at Salisbury and Ascot-at-Kempton ridden by the stable apprentice Eddie Grant. Chilcombe Belle took her name from Bill Stratton's training quarters not far from Upham on part of the infamous Twyford Down.

For such a modest performer without much of a pedigree, Chilcombe Belle, who is buried alongside Pneumatic at Ower Farm, did notably well as a broodmare. Four of her sons Turret (by Donore), Brookway (by Ennis), Bell-Tent (by Bivouac), and Spade Guinea (by Golden Dipper), all performed with credit. Ennis stood at a middle of the road fee of £400, but Lord Rosebery's pair, Donore at £148 and Bivouac at £98, were cheap Mentmore Stud stallions - and doubtless Norman Lonsdale, the manager of William Hill's Sezincote Stud in

Months of Misery Moments of Bliss

Gloucestershire, would have been open to offers for Golden Dipper's services!

Turret (Crocker Bulteel Stakes, Ascot), and Spade Guinea (Convivial Stakes, York), were sold as yearlings. Both were black type winners and the latter also finished third in the Royal Lodge Stakes at Ascot. Brookway was sold three times in as many years - he realised 550 guineas as a yearling at Newmarket, 725 guineas as a three-year-old at the Ascot Sales, and 675 guineas after winning a seller at Doncaster for the Upham stable as a four-year-old. That was in September 1969 and the following March he returned to Doncaster to finish third for his new connections in the Irish Sweeps Lincoln at odds of 100-1! Bell-Tent became a permanent appendage at Ower Farm where he was Bill's long serving hack - an awkward horse to ride with a very light mouth, no one else was very keen to exercise him. A gelding throughout his racing career he won ten times, the last of them as a seven-year-old when his owner-breeder-trainer saddled him to win the 1978 Daily Mirror Handicap at Epsom, the race preceding the Derby.

The third Ower Farm Stud family stems from the mare Dior (Dionisio - Bovington), whom Bill purchased as a yearling at Goffs in Ireland from her breeder Matthew F. Murphy for 600 guineas in September 1963. He was attracted to her as he had already won a race that season with her half-sister Ling Fing, but Dior herself only managed to win over hurdles. However, her final offspring for Bill and his partner Mrs Minnie Thomson, one of his earliest owners, proved to be the smart juvenile winner Diorina (by Manacle). Diorina in turn bred two useful daughters in Cheri Berry (by Air Trooper), and Hallorina (by Hallgate), both of whom scored five times.

Cheri Berry is the dam of Googly (by Sunley Builds), who became Bill's final winner when gaining the sixth victory of her career at Newbury in October 1993 - he kept a leg and leased the remainder to three friends, the mare running in the name of Alfred Lansley. A weekly visitor to Ower Farm to see Bill in his retirement, he lives not far away and the colours

Homebred Winners

(which were adapted from a set of silks belonging to a former patron of the stable), also did notably well with Single. Another joint owner in both horses was Sir Arthur Norman, a distinguished bomber pilot during the War and former chairman of De la Rue.

Just four days after Googly's farewell victory, she and her close relative Hallorina were consigned to the Newmarket Autumn Sales where the former realised 23,000 guineas and the latter 7,000 guineas - and their trainer was there to see them sold despite an attack of 'flu.

14

Reflections on a Trainer's Life

Bill Wightman has been going on to Stephen's Castle Down virtually every day during all seasons and in all weathers for more than half a century. Wonderful downland turf where good going can be guaranteed throughout the year, the gallops are horseshoe shaped and extend to two miles 'on the collar'. On chalk land they climb and undulate and, like all downland gallops, provide a much more searching test than the relatively flat terrain of Newmarket Heath - one canter on Stephen's Castle Down would be equivalent to at least two at Headquarters.

From the top side of the gallops there is a marvellous view over the valley with the paddocks of Egon Weinfeld's famous Meon Valley Stud clearly visible on the opposite bank. Nestling at the bottom is Dean Farm where Bill not only trained pre War, but where he also continued to live during his early bachelor years. In fact he laid the foundations of a stud there himself so the success of Meon Valley Stud gives him particular pleasure. In due course Evelyn Baring sold Dean Farm to Lord Penrhyn (whose father won the 1908 Grand National with Rubio), from whom Egon Weinfeld bought the property. Within a mile of Dean Farm, set amongst distant trees and hedgerows, is Michael Poland's Lower Preshaw House. How remarkable it is that Weinfeld and Poland should be the respective breeders of

Reflections on a Trainer's Life

the 1993 and 1994 King George VI and Queen Elizabeth Diamond Stakes winners Opera House and King's Theatre.

The gallops actually start at the bottom of the valley opposite Dean Farm beneath the hanger called Venus Drove and swing left-handed at about half-way as they climb to skirt the Bishop's Waltham road. Bill says that the terrain is absolutely ideal for doing long, steady canters. On the Ower Farm side of the road are the winter gallops which incorporate a two-year-old trial ground which was ploughed up to assist the War effort. Nowadays these workgrounds are largely obscured from view by substantial hedges, but forty years ago there was an uninhibited view from the road across this beautiful stretch of Hampshire countryside.

Certainly on a summer's morning with the skylarks climbing in a clear blue sky there is no place on earth that Bill would rather be than Stephen's Castle Down. But with racehorses there is always the unexpected to keep one on one's mettle and on the gallops dreams are made and illusions shattered. Sometimes there would be a pleasant surprise, perhaps a hitherto unpromising individual putting in a piece of good work way in excess of anything he or she has shown in the past. Conversely it could be a decidedly inept performance which caused an immediate rethink on some pending engagement. All these vicissitudes are just part and parcel of a trainer's life and merely emphasise that horses are not machines and that long term plans can all too easily go astray.

It was Bill who first described training as, 'months of misery, moments of bliss', a turn of phrase that has since been adopted by a number of his erstwhile colleagues. "The object of the exercise is to train winners and to me it didn't make any difference whether the objective was the Grand National or the July Cup. It's a matter of getting a horse fit and the technique is basically the same whether you are training for the flat or for jumping. Training a horse can be likened to driving a car but in slow motion. The difference is that in a car you have to anticipate what is going to happen in a split second - with a horse you are thinking in terms of weeks, or months, or even years.

"It's the hills that get them fit. This was brought home to me by Royal Tournament who was sent to me by his breeder C.W. Gordon. He wouldn't do a tap at home. In those days we had a sunken road up the middle of the horseshoe and one winter's day it was full of drifting snow. I was using Royal Tournament as a hack at the time and as I was on my own and he was a bit full of himself, I cantered on a bit up this particular piece of ground and soon he was blowing like a grampus. Usually he just wouldn't exert himself at home, but he had to in the snow and in this way I soon got him racing fit. There's no doubt that hills are an advantage, particularly with bad legged horses.

"The heart is a big muscle and that's where you slip up working good horses with bad horses. It's like tennis - a good player doesn't benefit from playing with a bad player but the bad player improves. When you work two horses together the good one is idling but the bad one is having to work hard to keep up. The vets say that unless a horse's heart is working at a minimum of three quarters' capacity you might as well not waste your time. Halloween, for example, would work over the full two miles twice a week.

"When I was younger and a horse was seriously injured I was much more inclined to say that he should be put down, whereas after being a prisoner of war I learnt to accept a lower standard - it made me more compassionate. I know it sounds corny but my primary concern has always been for the welfare of the horse. At the end of the day what is important is to bring about progress and improvement. We frequently jumped our flat horses over minor obstacles just to keep them interested. The reason why some horses are better jumpers than others is because they have good eyesight - no amount of schooling is going to make a blind horse jump well!

"If I was a horse I wouldn't want to be trained in some of these modern yards where the attitude is to win a race at all costs and then do the same with the next one regardless of the

Reflections on a Trainer's Life

consequences. The irony today is that everyone seems to be preaching animal rights and lack of cruelty yet the media are lauding the very people who do the exact opposite. In my opinion the Jockey Club is partly to blame because it gives licences to trainers who don't have any gallops. Obviously their horses can't be expected to run well first time out as they need two or three runs to get them racing fit."

Although he is not personally an advocate of interval training Bill would probably install an all weather gallop if he was training nowadays, despite the fact that they invariably need renewing every five years. In his experience they seldom fulfil the purpose for which they were intended. However, he admits an all weather strip would be very useful in preserving his hallowed turf during spells of very wet weather, "especially when my friends wanted to come and work their horses," he laughs. "But there has never been a time when I could not work on the grass here. Of course there is nothing new about interval training as this is what Paddy Prendergast used to do with all those top two-year-olds he brought over from Ireland.

"Berkshire, Wiltshire, Hampshire and Sussex are full of small training stables which have been in existence since the 1920s and the reason is the downland turf which has been left undisturbed for centuries, grazed only by sheep, rabbits and hares. Have I told you about my neighbour the late Bill Stratton who trained on Morestead Down? When he was not very well, he asked me over to watch his horses work. 'They are going 6 furlongs,' he said, 'the first four are on perfect ground, but the last two are a bit on the firm side - it's new ground and has only been down forty years!' He was perfectly serious. My two-year-old ground, which I re-seeded immediately after the War, is not as good as the ground that has never been ploughed.

"People sometimes ask me whether I would have preferred to train in a centre such as Newmarket or Lambourn. I'm a bit cynical about this and I shall get shot at for saying it but I know for a fact that people who are based in a training centre pick each others' brains. Now in my view, rightly or wrongly, the

Months of Misery Moments of Bliss

only person you should consult if you have a problem is your vet. I was lucky to have started with the great G.P. Male from Reading, followed by his successor Peter Scott-Dunn, an equally brilliant man with an international practice. People also assume that it must be much easier from a labour point of view to be in a training centre, but I can honestly say it's never been a problem and I never had to advertise for staff.

"Of course being out on one's own does have obvious advantages if you are a betting stable. I have never regarded myself as a betting trainer and the fact that I have made money from betting over the years is not the point. But I have always looked upon betting as a minor part of racing and fortunately I am not excitable enough to get carried away by it. You have to remember that all trainers are dependent on owners and no trainer worth his salt would want to spoil a horse for the sake of winning a bet. But I have never been averse to telling an owner who didn't bet to have a little on when everything was in the horse's favour. Everything in moderation. It was Les Hall, 'the wizard of Winchester', whom I first met training at Northolt, who used to say, 'Some trainers race to bet, and some bet to race.'

"I have always been an advocate of ante-post betting. When the bookmakers make their book months before the Lincoln, for example, they may quote your horse at 66-1 without having a clue as to whether or not it will run. So you have £200 each way or whatever. Then just as soon as it becomes known that the horse has been doing some good work at home and is sure to run with a top jockey booked to ride, the price shortens dramatically and this enables you to lay it off with your bookmaker. In other words you can have your bet for nothing - it's a wonderful system.

"Training is a routine job seven days a week. Wednesdays and Saturdays were usually our work days. I always went out with the horses and I always rode out. There was none of this driving around with a car telephone. I rode all sorts of hacks, striped ones, spotted ones, bob tailed ones, but usually a

Reflections on a Trainer's Life

racehorse, sometimes a hunter. If I was not going racing I would ride two lots. Over the years two lots developed into three lots not because the stable was expanding but through sheer economics. The lads started every morning at seven o'clock. Together with my head man I would arrange who rode what the previous evening when it was posted on the stable board. First lot would pull out at about 7.30 am. In the really hot weather in the summer we would start that much earlier. The unmarried lads lived in a bothy with a housekeeper to look after them while the others were dotted around locally. In the old days they used to come to work on bicycles - there was the odd motor-bike but cars were very rare."

One aspect of training racehorses which has changed dramatically during Bill's long innings is feeding. "Nowadays everything is standardised and nuts form the basis of most horses' feed. In the old days the head lad had a much more responsible job mixing up the food individually. It was mostly oats and bran and we cooked a hot linseed mash twice a week. The lads were always at it - they had to go out to find the wood to light the boiler. Of course good quality hay is paramount and so too is water. If your horses are out of form for any length of time a bad batch of hay or oats is as likely as not to be the main culprit. It can have a devastating effect. I remember Staff Ingham's head lad telling me just how worried they were when the stable was out of form once. They were so desperate to pinpoint a reason they even began to think that they were overgirthing their runners! Nowadays they invariably put it down to the virus.

"But any trainer is only as good as his horses. I always think it is remarkable that we had any winners at all. Stanley Cayzer was the best sort of owner you could possibly have. A charming man he used to say every summer, 'I want to buy three yearlings and I will pay so much for them.' So you were able to go shopping. There is no comparison between a struggling trainer and an established trainer in the top flight - it's as different as chalk from cheese.

"I never used to socialise on the racecourse. I always got there in time to do my job and left immediately afterwards. There was so much more to be done at home. I've always run the show myself. Every time one had a runner it was a great thrill although the anticipation might be more a fear of running badly than winning. I think trainers today are inclined to be too greedy, they run their horses too often. I suppose my philosophy to training, which is a worrying job, is to take advantage of any opportunity that occurs. It's best not to tell the owner too much, but if you feel a horse is too high in the handicap, run him on the sort of going that you know doesn't suit! That's not cheating, it's management.

"When I was young I used to ride out with a long-tom but I soon realised that was not the way to get the best out of horses. You have to go along with some of these old characters, they're all different - in that way you get a lot more mileage on the clock. To get the best out of them they need to enjoy themselves. But training is not the game it was, most of us old timers agree that we have seen the best of it. When I started training ponies my training fees were £2-10s-0d a week - 50 shillings. I remember when I put my training fees up from £12-10s-0d to £13-0s-0d a week, old Flo Prior, who was a keen businesswoman, said she wasn't going to pay! I was very flattered when Charlie Gordon, the breeder of Royal Tournament, asked me to train a horse for his wife. Then he asked me what I charged saying that he had trained with Jack Jarvis for years and had never paid more than £1-0s-0d per day. But I had to point out that it was more nowadays!"

The veteran Hampshire trainer has always been a great believer in getting the right jockey for a particular horse. The high profile combination was Fred Winter and Halloween, but Bill cites many other examples under both Rules, including Doug Smith and Pneumatic, Michael Scudamore and Hilarion, Pat Eddery and Single. And the factor that made any one pair compatible is style. "With Pneumatic you had to 'catch him right', particularly at the start. In his day it was the old barrier

Reflections on a Trainer's Life

start and why do you think Gordon Richards rode so many winners? Because he always got well away. And why did he get well away? Because the starter saw him well away - it was the reward for being a great champion. I suppose stalls were inevitable but I still think long distance flat races should be started in the old fashioned way - often jockeys like to drop one in behind."

It was an incident at the old barrier start at Kempton Park which resulted in Bill making the first of just a handful of appearances up before the stewards. "My filly had reared up and unseated Bill Anderson down at the start when she was frightened by one horse kicking out at another runner. The Queen's racing manager Charles Moore was in the chair at the time and he blamed me entirely for the whole incident. He never gave me a chance to explain. It reminded me of the time that Charlie Smirke cut the wires of Eph Smith's hearing aid just before a stewards' enquiry!

"On another occasion I was running Halloween at Newbury and he used to get a bit on his toes at the races. The facilities in the saddling boxes were rather inadequate in those days so I went and asked the stewards' secretary if I could saddle him in the stable yard and he went to get permission from the clerk of the course Geoffrey Freer. As he leant out of the weighing room window, I heard him ask the 'stipe' who it was. 'Bill Wightman' came the reply. 'Well he's alright but the answer's no!' "

15

A Team Effort

"It is absolutely essential to have a loyal and happy staff," says Bill Wightman, "who not only understand what it is you want them to do but are prepared to do everything humanly possible to achieve that goal. Inevitably the great majority of horses you train are not going to be anything special but all my lads used to take just as much care and trouble with a 'no hoper' as with a good horse. Looking back I cannot over emphasise how fortunate I was to have two men like Bill Nash and Bill Anderson, both of whom worked for me for the best part of 50 years. They were indispensable."

The three Bills, now all in their eighties, are a unique triumvirate. Remarkably all three come from in and around London, Bill Wightman from Streatham, Bill Nash from Brentford, and Bill Anderson from Hackney. They have all loved anything to do with horses since they were youngsters and there is no doubting the high regard and the mutual respect that they have for one another. Nash and Anderson, who still live no distance from Upham, have no hesitation in saying that they have had a marvellous life working with racehorses in general and with the guv'nor in particular and they would do exactly the same thing all over again given the opportunity. Their admiration for Bill Wightman as a man and as an employer knows no bounds.

A Team Effort

It was at Bill Nash's suggestion that Bill Anderson left Charles Elsey's stable at Malton shortly after the war to come south and join Bill Wightman's small team at Ower Farm, Upham. The two men had been apprentices together at Chantilly in France during the 1920s. Bill Nash served his time with Percy Carter and Bill Anderson with Claude Halsey. From just a handful of rides Bill Nash gained two successes, at Saint-Cloud and Maisons-Laffitte, before troubled by increasing weight. Bill Anderson became an established jockey in his own right with a substantial tally of winners to his credit on both the Parisian tracks and in the south of France. Whilst attached to Marcel Boussac's stable he rode regularly alongside such stars as Charlie Elliot, whom he would meet up with again on joining Bill Wightman, and Rae 'Le Crocodile' Johnstone. That was a golden era when the Boussac colours were carried by such celebrities as Djebel, Pharis and Tourbillon, and as likely as not Bill Anderson rode one of the pacemakers.

Bill Nash has an even longer association with Ower Farm than the guv'nor for he went there from Stanley Wootton's Epsom yard in 1937 when Harry Lowe was still training for Sir Walden Chilcott. Based at Lee-on-Solent with the Fleet Air Arm for much of the War, Bill rode such stars as Kingsfold and Halloween in most of their serious work. However, he rates Our Note (Royal Note - Our Kretchen) as potentially the best horse he ever rode on the gallops. This American bred, who was owned by Edward Benjamin, was beaten a neck by Swing Easy for the 1970 New Stakes, Royal Ascot, but was repatriated to the USA at the end of the season.

It was fortuitous that Bill Anderson managed to get himself and his young family out of France before the German occupation; he arrived back in England after travelling from Paris down to Bordeaux and then on to Biarritz. An electrician in the RAF during the War, he spent some time in North Africa and while in Algiers managed to augment his tally of winners to about three hundred. Perhaps the most memorable of them for Bill Wightman was Evelyn Baring's S.E.A.C. on whom he

Months of Misery Moments of Bliss

defeated Gordon Richards by a head at Windsor one November afternoon in 1947. Of all his favourites at Ower Farm, he puts old Pneumatic high on the list.

Bill Anderson's daughter Lillian married the stable's long serving travelling head lad Geoff Yates. He became a familiar sight in the paddock; always well turned out, he made sure that the stable's smart grey or navy blue paddock sheets were retrieved without incident. Having served in the King's Troop, RHA, he succeeded the bespectacled figure of Don de Silva who used to lead Halloween round all those years ago. Nowadays Geoff Yates, who became head lad on Bill Nash's retirement, works on the racecourse where he assists in the veterinary examination box taking post race samples.

Some mornings Bill Anderson would ride work on a succession of horses and he and Bill Nash were still riding out on Stephen's Castle Down well into their seventies. While Bill Anderson rode regularly in public for the stable on the flat his counterpart jumping was Desmond Dartnall. Brought up in the world of flapping he was apprenticed to Bill Wightman back in the old days and rode pony winners for him. "He was a jolly good chap, a very competent jockey ('nobody rode Kandy Boy better'), and was of enormous help to me". Subsequently Desmond Dartnall trained in his own right, first at Condicote, Stow-on-the-Wold, and later near Chepstow. It was very much a family affair as his two sons Gerald and Victor both rode as professionals for the stable - in March 1970 Gerald scored on Kingdom for Bill Wightman at Sandown Park. Desmond Dartnall was still at Condicote when David Nicholson embarked upon his training career there.

"The main reason I employed people like Bill Anderson and Des Dartnall was because I needed good work riders. The skill of the work rider is to keep the moderate horse on the bit, otherwise like humans they are disappointed. A lead horse can't do everything and you pair your horses off, mostly by age groups, together with their riders. You wouldn't work a 5 furlong horse with a two mile horse. You have to remember

A Team Effort

that in Newmarket few of the lads used to ride work, it was mostly done by jockeys. At the top level you had Cecil Boyd-Rochfort who would employ a gang of jockeys to ride work and they would ride one and then get into a car to go back and ride another. They would probably each ride six lots in a morning with Bruce Hobbs standing down at the start with a long-tom to ensure that they got off.

"We always took a certain number of apprentices, a lot of local lads of school leaving age used to apply. The only qualification was that they had to be small and under a certain weight. They did not need to have riding experience. There was also a contact in Ireland who used to arrange to send good boys over. You would pay him £10 and say you wanted two or three and they duly arrived. I had some smashing chaps. They signed on for a five year apprenticeship and were clothed (they all rode out in breeches and caps), fed, and housed, and received pocket money on a sliding scale."

Boxing was popular with a number of the lads, amongst them Brian Lawrence who came from Woolston, Southampton. A younger brother of ABA champion Ken Lawrence, Brian was the stable lads' 6st 7lb open boxing champion - in those days the stable lads' boxing championship was held annually in Marlborough. He had never ridden a horse when he joined Bill Wightman in 1950 aged fifteen, but he became a very useful jump jockey, gaining a major success eight years later on Oscar Wilde in the Welsh Grand National at Chepstow. Brian Lawrence, who did a lot of travelling with horses for the stable, was a strong rider seen to particular advantage over fences.

Another local lad to make the grade as a National Hunt jockey was Trevor Pink, whose grandfather was a builder and undertaker from Bishop's Waltham. He served his time with Bill Wightman and looked after Kingsfold early in his career. After a two year break from Ower Farm he returned to make his name over jumps, establishing a particular rapport with the enigmatic Roxburgh. Tragically, Trevor Pink died as the result of a fall in a novices' 'chase at Taunton in February 1965 when riding for a West Country permit holder.

A number of Bill's apprentices rode winners on the flat, amongst them Donald Gale, Ken Wright, Pat Brownsea, Eddie Grant, Micky Ginn, Hughie Grattan, Gerry McCann, Tom O'Sullivan and Steve Woolley. He has particular reason to remember Donald Gale as the 20-year-old from Barrow in Furness gained the first victory of his career when winning on his own filly Cadenabbia (High Profit - Genoa), who broke her duck at Bath in August 1951. The owner-trainer must have been feeling in particularly generous mood after his own wedding to Antoinette Jones in Winchester just two weeks earlier as he had promised the young apprentice a new motor-bike if he managed to win!

Like the Manton maestro George Todd, Bill was never averse to putting up apprentices, but, as he says, there is so much luck involved. Very often there are no suitable rides in the stable for an apprentice and when there are not every owner is prepared to give them a chance. However, he was responsible for Karen Wiltshire, the very first professional woman rider to win a flat race in the UK. "She served her apprenticeship with me; when she came for an interview she said she wanted to ride a winner." She duly went into the record books when scoring on The Goldstone at Salisbury in September 1978.

Another familiar face both on and off the racecourse who has shared many of Bill Wightman's trials and tribulations is Diana Roth. One day at Fontwell Park, Sam Sheppard, who had a horse in training at the time at Ower Farm and was to run The Thoroughbred Breeders' Association, told Diana that Bill Wightman was looking for a secretary and she joined him in September 1968. For the first ten-and-a-half years she worked full time, riding out, organising the office, driving to race meetings, liaising between the lads, compiling catalogue details, in fact helping out in every way possible. Her involvement with the stable continued until his retirement albeit by then she was working on a part time, freelance basis.

A Team Effort

One November day in 1975, Diana, Bill and Tom O'Sullivan were involved in an amusing incident en route to seeing her filly Catamaran (Lauso - Oceania) compete at Haydock Park as the trainer explains. "It was my first run in a new Jaguar XJS, which was then one of the very first to be registered and at Cirencester we found we were being tailed by a police car. But all they wanted to know was why my registration number BW65 (Bishop's Waltham 65 was my old telephone number) had been on an Austin only the previous week! After a hectic drive through the rain with major road works on the way, we eventually arrived at Haydock about half an hour before the race, but Catamaran had been declared to run by the travelling head lad. Catamaran duly won!"

Breakfast between first and second lots is always an important item on the agenda for any racing stable, providing an ideal opportunity to compare notes. Diana recalls that one topic which invariably cropped up at Ower Farm was where a particular horse was best handicapped. In those days handicapping was shared between a panel of handicappers so horses could be treated very differently according to which handicapper was responsible for the weights in any particular race. Of course with centralised handicapping that loophole has been closed, thereby removing a lot of the fun and skill in placing horses.

For Diana Roth her most memorable day's racing was when Privateer won the William Hill Portland Handicap. It was also a very profitable afternoon for Bill as he backed Privateer in a 64-1 double with Silver Birch, winner of the Princess Mary Nursery. She was trained by his old friend Tom Waugh, whom he had first got to know when Tom was assistant to Fred Butters at Kingsclere. Silver Birch was owned by Mrs Rosemary Newton for whom Bill was to win races with Silver Birch's son Golden Birch. Diana also recalls Bill's bete noire Tracklecka winning a seller on the July Course at Newmarket. "He had two left front feet and raced barefoot - he could not be shod in front or he would have cut his joints to ribbons."

Months of Misery Moments of Bliss

Few people will have had a closer insight into Bill's technique as a trainer than Diana Roth especially from a book point of view. She says that he studied both the Form Book and the Stud Book closely and this was very evident when he went to the yearling sales - his catalogue was always marked up very carefully. If she had to put a finger on his greatest talent as a trainer she thinks it was probably his ability to assess a horse's best distance. Having determined that, his modus operandi with an animal that showed some ability was to identify a worthwhile prize at some future date rather than just going for a suitable run of the mill race when winning made such a comparatively small contribution to an owner's overall costs.

16

The longest serving Trainer

No great fanfare of trumpets heralded Bill Wightman's retirement. No sooner had Googly (Sunley Builds - Cheri Berry), whom he bred himself in partnership with Minnie Thomson, come from last to first to win the PCL Handicap at Newbury on Thursday, October 21, 1993, thus providing John Reid with his first ever century, than he announced that she was his final runner. "I've put my guns away, I've had the best shooting," he said at the time. The news imparted in a characteristically low key manner took a while to sink in, but the fact of the matter was there would be no more winners trained by W.G.R. Wightman, Upham - at least not under Rules. For a coterie of friends, supporters and professional colleagues present it was much more than just a nostalgic moment - there was a sense of loss which is difficult to put into words.

When Bill announced his retirement aged seventy-nine he was the last of the current trainers in Britain to have started training before the Second World War - and he was also the senior member of that fraternity (in terms of years holding a licence) under both Rules, which is probably a unique achievement. He had held seniority for six years following the retirement of Sir Guy Cunard in 1987. Cunard, who was the top point-to-point rider of his day, started to train his own horses under Rules in 1932, sixteen years before the introduction of permits for those training their own horses or those belonging to their immediate family. Only later did he become a public trainer but never on a large scale.

The leading trainer of the 1990s to be training pre-war was the late Fulke Walwyn, whose Mont Tremblant spent three days at Ower Farm prior to his victory in the 1952 Cheltenham Gold Cup because the gallops at Lambourn were frozen solid. Bill remembers it well, "He cantered up my best summer gallop during a hard frost but the ground was perfect as there was such a thick covering of grass." Fulke Walwyn first took out a licence for the 1939 season in Lambourn and he was still training there when he died in February 1990 at the age of eighty. The licence was taken over for the next few years by his wife Cath. That fifty-one year span was just bettered by another top jumps' trainer in Neville Crump - the Middleham trainer embarked upon his career at Upavon in Wiltshire in 1937 and retired in 1989.

Bill's successor as the country's longest serving trainer became Jack O'Donoghue and he too gained his most important success with a famous jumper. From his Priory Stables, Reigate, Jack enjoyed his greatest single moment of glory in 1951 when Nickel Coin became the last mare to win the Grand National. An Irishman, he had saddled his first winner in November 1946. He also trained Gay Record, whose wayward disposition was apparently not suited to the regime at Peter Cazalet's Fairlawne yard, to score a one hundredth victory for the Queen Mother.

Jack O'Donoghue was still training winners in 1995 at the age of eighty-eight, but he is still younger than Norah Wilmot, who was only four days short of her ninety-first birthday when her licence expired in January 1980. Norah Wilmot, who trained for the Queen and the Queen Mother, had taken over the running of the Binfield Grove stable near Bracknell, close to Ascot racecourse, following the death of her father Sir Robert Wilmot in 1931, but was not officially recognised as a trainer until 1966. One of the head lads to hold the licence on her behalf was Wally Swash and Bill lodged with him when he had been head lad to Laing Ward!

Bill always used to say that he would continue training so long as he enjoyed it and was in good health with the proviso that it did not cost him too much - latterly he owned most of the horses himself in partnership with various friends. When finally deciding to draw stumps, he had every intention of making a complete break and he set the wheels in motion to sell his yard and the 300 acre farm that goes with it. However, when Bill Smith asked him to take some broodmares at livery he decided to stay put - Fulke Walwyn's former stable jockey stood Sunley Builds, sire of Googly, at his Kelanne House Stud no distance away at Hambledon.

There has never been any cause to regret that decision and Bill remains extremely self sufficient, not that there seems to be any shortage of visitors to offer a helping hand or pass the time of day! One of his former employees to whom he is exceedingly grateful is Sue Eburn. She volunteered to let her own house and move into a house in the yard at Ower Farm so that she could keep an eye on this sprightly octogenarian and help out on the domestic front at the same time; that is when she is not busy working at Winchester's County Library headquarters.

Although Bill has forsaken two of his favourite pastimes, hunting and shooting, it would seem that horses and dogs are reluctant to give him up. True he no longer breeds his beloved labradors but only recently he procured a golden labrador from an animal sanctuary ostensibly as a guard dog. Evidently Jasper is a great success in his new role although the postman cannot be relied upon to place the mail through the office window any more! Jasper has also found the wide variety of wild life that frequents the garden surrounding the house and stables a never ending source of entertainment, much to his owner's amusement.

Months of Misery Moments of Bliss

Ower Farm without horses would be unthinkable. One moment there are a couple of pretty girls coming up the drive on their point-to-pointers to request permission to do a bit of work on Stephen's Castle Down and the next Bill is discussing with Richard Newman how well one of the young horses jumped round the bull-ring as they refer to the schooling ground at the back of the house. Richard, who rode winners for Bill Wightman and for Bob Turnell and is a most accomplished horseman, served his time at Ower Farm and returned there after an interim period in Ireland.

Pottering about the stable yard, Bill checks over the other inmates. His enthusiasm is undiminished and he takes just as much time and trouble with his old point-to-pointer Popeswood (Nicholas Bill - Villarrica) as he ever did with some of the more famous inmates of these picturesque flint and brick stables. In 1995 Popeswood, who joined Bill's band of pensioners to ensure that Nick Hitchins' gelding had a good retirement home, won the local Hambledon Cup which his trainer had won previously back in 1954. Another of his charges is the homebred Roadrunner (Sunley Builds - Derraleena). This gelding is named after a shop in London owned by Bill's daughter Dulce, which specialises in in-line roller skates. Not only does he take the greatest interest in her business career (she recently opened another shop in Brighton), but is also a proud grandfather.

Qualified with the local Hursley and Hambledon Hunt, Popeswood won two open point-to-points during the 1994 season. One of them was at Barbury Castle within a mile of two famous training establishments, Manton and Ogbourne Maisey on the Marlborough Downs. Here Bill Wightman was amazed to discover that the estate on which the point-to-point is held was managed by Desmond Dartnall's son Victor. In fact it was Victor who was responsible for resurrecting the course. And that brings one back to the very beginning of this remarkable story of a master trainer of racehorses who remains firmly ensconced in his Hampshire idyll.

Chronological List of Winners
(National Hunt Winners in Italics)

Year	Owner	Winner	Location	Jockey
1937				
May 18	G.H. Rumsey	SUNNY PEACE	Buckfastleigh (chase)	B. Hobbs
Sept 1	G.H. Rumsey	SUNNY PEACE	Totnes (chase)	A. Scratchley
Sept 14	W.G.R. Wightman	AUTUMN	Warwick	Mr. P.Herbert
1938				
May 6	Major Durham Matthews	GREAT BARTON	Ripon	Mr. E. Underdown
May 20	Major Durham Matthews	GREAT BARTON	Lingfield Park	Mr. E. Underdown
Aug 1	Major Durham Matthews	GREAT BARTON	Ripon	H. Blackshaw
Aug 13	G.H. Rumsey	BURMAN	Windsor	W. Rickaby
1946				
Nov 15	*Contessa di Sant' Elia*	*SOUTHBOROUGH*	*Wincanton (chase)*	*D. Dartnall*
1947				
Nov 13	E.B. Baring	S.E.A.C	Windsor	W. Anderson
Nov 27	*Contessa di Sant' Elia*	*SOUTHBOROUGH*	*Wincanton (chase)*	*P. Lay*
1948				
Jan 3	*W.G.R. Wightman*	*PETROGRAD*	*Plumpton (chase)*	*D. Dartnall*
Jan 16	*E.B. Baring*	*SUN CHEER*	*Lingfield Park (hurdle)*	*D. Dartnall*
Jan 22	*Contessa di Sant' Elia*	*SUN*	*Wincanton (chase)*	*D. Dartnall*
Feb 7	*Contessa di Sant' Elia*	*SUN*	*Windsor (chase)*	*D. Dartnall*
Mar 27	*Contessa di Sant' Elia*	*SOUTHBOROUGH*	*Plumpton (chase)*	*Cmdr. R. Courage*
Apr 9	E.B. Baring	FINAL SCORE	Hurst Park	D. Greening
July 7	E.B. Baring	FINAL SCORE	Salisbury	E.C. Elliot
July 20	E.B. Baring	WHITEBEAM	Folkestone	H. Packham
Aug 9	E.B. Baring	TOM CRIBB	Nottingham	E. Mercer
Aug 10	E.B. Baring	FINAL SCORE	Nottingham	E.C. Elliot
Aug 31	E.B. Baring	WHITEBEAM	Lewes	H. Packham
Sept 20	*F.E. Frampton*	*KITSON*	*Fontwell Park (hurdle)*	*D. Dartnall*
Sept 21	E.B. Baring	TOM CRIBB	Leicester	E. Mercer
Oct 9	E.B. Baring	S.E.A.C	Chepstow	C. Orton
Nov 12	Contessa di Sant' Elia	KANDY BOY	Liverpool	H. Packham
1949				
Mar 17	*Mrs. M. Glenister*	*TARKA*	*Wincanton (hurdle)*	*D. Dartnall*
Apr 16	*F.E. Frampton*	*KITSON*	*Plumpton (chase)*	*D. Dartnall*
Aug 3	E.B. Baring	S.E.A.C	Brighton	P. Tomlin
Sept 6	E.B. Baring	DEVONIC	Chepstow	G. Richards
Sept 20	E.B. Baring	DEVONIC	Leicester	G. Richards
Oct 22	Mrs. M. Glenister	TARKA	Doncaster	W. Snaith

Months of Misery Moments of Bliss

Nov 11	E.B. Baring	ROCKAWAY	Liverpool	R. Bradley
Nov 19	E.B. Baring	ROCKAWAY	Lingfield Park	W. Anderson
Dec 27	Mrs. M. Glenister	TARKA	Wincanton (hurdle)	D. Dartnall

1950

Feb 3	Contessa di Sant' Elia	KANDY BOY	Windsor (hurdle)	R. Turnell
Mar 4	Contessa di Sant' Elia	SOUTHBOROUGH	Kempton Park (chase)	R. Turnell
Apr 1	Mrs. M. Glenister	TARKA	Newbury	R. Bradley
May 13	E.B. Baring	DEVONIC	Worcester	H. Packham
June 10	E.B. Baring	DEVONIC	Worcester	H. Packham
June 24	W.H. Whitaker	FAIR SUNSHINE	Leicester	F. Gurney
June 26	Contessa di Sant' Elia	KANDY BOY	Brighton	H. Packham
July 18	W.H. Whitaker	FAIR SUNSHINE	Sandown Park	H. Packham
Aug 7	S. Bull	BEN MOOR II	Epsom	W. Anderson
Aug 12	S. Bull	SANDASTRE	Lewes	G. Richards
Aug 28	E.B. Baring	LYCASTE	Birmingham	E. Smith
Sept 11	E.B. Baring	LYCASTE	Wolverhampton	E. Smith
Sept 21	S. Bull	BEN MOOR II	Wincanton (hurdle)	D. Dartnall
Oct 9	S. Bull	BEN MOOR II	Fontwell Park (hurdle)	D. Dartnall
Dec 9	Contessa di Sant' Elia	SOUTHBOROUGH	Windsor (chase)	D. Dartnall

1951

Feb 3	Capt. R. Smalley	HALLOWEEN	Windsor (chase)	Owner
Feb 16	Capt. R. Smalley	HALLOWEEN	Sandown Park (chase)	Owner
Feb 28	Contessa di Sant' Elia	KANDY BOY	Windsor (chase)	D. Dartnall
Mar 5	Capt. R. Smalley	HALLOWEEN	Worcester (chase)	Owner
Mar 16	Capt. R. Smalley	HALLOWEEN	Sandown Park (chase)	Owner
Apr 25	Capt. R. Smalley	HALLOWEEN	Cheltenham (chase)	Owner
May 18	E.B. Baring	DEVONIC	Lingfield Park	E. Mercer
May 28	Contessa di Sant' Elia	AKARA	Wolverhampton	E. Mercer
June 23	S. Bull	BEN MOOR II	Worcester	R. Bradley
July 19	E.B. Baring	RUSHCUTTER	Bath	G. Richards
July 23	E.B. Baring	DEVONIC	Folkestone	E. Mercer
July 24	Contessa di Sant' Elia	AKARA	Folkestone	E. Mercer
Aug 6	E.B. Baring	DEVONIC	Chepstow	T. Carter
Aug 15	W.G.R. Wightman	CADENABBIA	Bath	D. Gale
Sept 13	Major M.J. Gilliat	KANDY BOY	Fontwell Park (chase)	Major R. Hastings
Oct 17	E.B. Baring	DEVONIC	Cheltenham (hurdle)	T. Molony
Dec 21	Capt. R. Smalley	CLAY PIT	Hurst Park (hurdle)	D. Dartnall
Dec 29	Contessa di Sant' Elia	HALLOWEEN	Newbury (chase)	Capt. R. Smalley

1952

Jan 9	Major M.J. Gilliat	KANDY BOY	Plumpton (chase)	D. Dartnall
Feb 22	Contessa di Sant' Elia	HALLOWEEN	Newbury (chase)	Capt. R. Smalley
Mar 8	Contessa di Sant' Elia	HALLOWEEN	Hurst Park (chase)	F. Winter
Apr 18	Mrs. L.W. Smith	KINGSFOLD	Newbury	E. Smith
May 7	Mrs. L.W. Smith	KINGSFOLD	Sandown Park	E.C. Elliot
May 10	Contessa di Sant' Elia	AKARA	Chepstow (d-h)	H. Packham
	Mrs. W.G.R. Wightman	NOTARY	Chepstow	G. Richards

Chronological List of Winners

July 14	B.F. Butler	THRIFTY LAD	Birmingham	D. Gale
Aug 16	B.F. Butler	THRIFTY LAD	Newbury	D. Gale
Sept 25	P. Hatvany	QUEEN'S BENCH	Ascot	E. Mercer
Oct 22	Contessa di Sant' Elia	HALLOWEEN	Hurst Park (chase)	F. Winter
Oct 24	P. Hatvany	CHIVALRY	Newbury	L. Piggott
	Mrs. L.W. Smith	KINGSFOLD	Newbury	W. Rickaby
Oct 27	Contessa di Sant' Elia	AMAPA	Alexandra Park	D. Smith
Nov 20	Major M.J. Gilliat	KANDY BOY	Hurst Park (chase)	D. Dartnall
Nov 29	Contessa di Sant' Elia	HALLOWEEN	Kempton Park (chase)	F. Winter
Dec 26	Contessa di Sant' Elia	HALLOWEEN	Kempton Park (chase)	F. Winter

1953

Jan 31	Contessa di Sant' Elia	HALLOWEEN	Windsor (chase)	F. Winter
Mar 14	J.A. Leavett-Shenley	MINIMAX	Sandown Park (chase)	Owner
Apr 16	Contessa di Sant' Elia	AMAPA	Newmarket	E. Smith
Apr 20	P. Hatvany	PAST LOVE	Wolverhampton	W. Rickaby
Apr 29	Mrs. L.W. Smith	KINGSFOLD	Newmarket	E. Smith
May 12	Mrs. L.W. Smith	KINGSFOLD	Newmarket	E. Smith
June 25	Mrs. W.G.R. Wightman	PNEUMATIC	Newbury	D. Smith
July 7	Contessa di Sant' Elia	KANDY BOY	Salisbury	K. Wright
Sept 28	Contessa di Sant' Elia	KANDY BOY	Fontwell Park (chase)	E. Reavey
Oct 29	Contessa di Sant' Elia	AMAPA	Newmarket (d-h)	E. Smith
Nov 5	Contessa di Sant' Elia	HALLOWEEN	Wincanton (chase)	T. Molony

1954

Apr 7	J.A. Leavett-Shenley	FIRE PRINCE	Sandown Park (chase)	Owner
June 14	Miss F.M. Prior	FELICITY	Leicester	W. Rickaby
July 23	Mrs. J.M. Stephenson	HILARION	Hurst Park	D. Smith
Sept 27	E.B. Baring	FINAL COMMAND	Birmingham	D. Smith
Oct 18	Contessa di Sant' Elia	PNEUMATIC	Wolverhampton	D. Smith
Nov 11	Contessa di Sant' Elia	HALLOWEEN	Cheltenham (chase)	F. Winter
Dec 16	Contessa di Sant' Elia	HALLOWEEN	Sandown Park (chase)	F. Winter
Dec 27	Contessa di Sant' Elia	HALLOWEEN	Kempton Park (chase)	F. Winter

1955

Feb 16	J.A. Leavett-Shenley	FIRE PRINCE	Newbury (chase)	Owner
Feb 26	Contessa di Sant' Elia	HALLOWEEN	Kempton Park (chase)	F. Winter
Mar 14	J.A. Edney	ANTHONY WAYNE	Warwick (hurdle)	M. Scudamore
Apr 1	Mrs. J.M. Stephenson	HILARION	Newbury (d-h)	H. Packham
Apr 21	J.A. Edney	ANTHONY WAYNE	Wincanton (hurdle)	J. Maguire
Apr 22	Lord Hampden	TREETOPS HOTEL	Sandown Park	W. Rickaby
May 18	Lord Hampden	TREETOPS HOTEL	Salisbury	E. Smith
June 20	Contessa di Sant' Elia	PNEUMATIC	Folkestone	D. Smith
July 9	E.B. Baring	FINAL LINE	Sandown Park	D. Smith
	J.A. Leavett-Shenley	FLORIDO II	Worcester	Owner
July 21	E.B. Baring	FINAL LINE	Kempton Park	D. Smith
June 25	Miss F.M. Prior	GREENSWARD	Lingfield Park	D. Smith
July 23	Mrs. C.H. Feilden	PHOENIX PARK	Worcester	D. Ryan
	Exors of late W.F. Stratton	FABRICATION	Worcester	D. Ryan

Months of Misery Moments of Bliss

Aug 20	Miss F.M. Prior	GREENSWARD	Lingfield Park	W. Rickaby
Aug 31	Mrs. C.H. Feilden	FINALITY	Bath	W. Rickaby
Sept 13	Mrs. C.H. Feilden	PHOENIX PARK	Wolverhampton	D. Ryan
Oct 4	Mrs. J.M. Stephenson	HILARION	Fontwell Park (hurdle)	M. Scudamore
Oct 17	Contessa di Sant' Elia	PNEUMATIC	Wolverhampton	D. Smith
Nov 23	J.A. Leavett-Shenley	FIRE PRINCE	Kempton Park (chase)	F. Winter
Nov 24	J.A. Edney	ANTHONY WAYNE	Kempton Park (hurdle)	J. Maguire
Dec 10	J. Corbett	HALVIEW PET	Newbury (hurdle)	D. Ancil
	J.A. Leavett-Shenley	FIRE PRINCE	Newbury (chase)	Owner
Dec 27	J.A. Edney	ANTHONY WAYNE	Kempton Park (hurdle)	J. Maguire

1956

May 17	Miss F.M. Prior	ABERDOVEY	Bath	D. Greening
May 30	Mrs. G.B. Hunt	PHOENIX PARK	Windsor	D. Greening
July 19	Contessa di Sant' Elia	PNEUMATIC	Bath	L. Piggott
July 30	Lord Hampden	FULL MOUTH	Alexandra Park	D. Smith
Aug 22	Contessa di Sant' Elia	PNEUMATIC	Sandown Park	R. Williams
Aug 24	Miss F. M. Prior	ABERDOVEY	Lingfield Park	D. Smith
Sept 4	Contessa di Sant' Elia	PNEUMATIC	Lewes	R. Williams
Oct 25	Contessa di Sant' Elia	PNEUMATIC	Newbury	D. Smith
Nov 17	Miss F.M. Prior	ABERDOVEY	Lingfield Park	D.W. Morris
Nov 21	Contessa di Sant' Elia	HILARION	Newbury (hurdle)	M. Scudamore

1957

Jan 18	Contessa di Sant' Elia	HILARION	Sandown Park (hurdle)	M. Scudamore
Jan 26	J.A. Edney	ANTHONY WAYNE	Kempton Park (hurdle)	J. Maguire
Mar 15	Contessa di Sant' Elia	HILARION	Hurst Park (hurdle)	M. Scudamore
Apr 17	J.A. Edney	ANTHONY WAYNE	Cheltenham (hurdle)	J. Maguire
May 22	Miss F.M. Prior	DROVER'S WAY	Salisbury	W. Rickaby
June 24	E.B. Baring	PENULTIMATE	Birmingham	D. Smith
July 2	E.B. Baring	PENULTIMATE	Wolverhampton	F. Durr
July 9	Miss F. M. Prior	CLOVER HONEY	Salisbury	W. Rickaby
July 11	Mrs. M.D. Herniman	ROSE KNIGHT	Salisbury	W. Rickaby
July 18	Contessa di Sant' Elia	PNEUMATIC	Bath	J. Mercer
Aug 14	Contessa di Sant' Elia	PNEUMATIC	Sandown Park	D. Smith
Oct 24	Contessa di Sant' Elia	PNEUMATIC	Newbury	D. Smith
Dec 12	W.G.R. Wightman	SARAH'S BOY	Sandown Park (hurdle)	G. Slack

1958

Jan 11	Contessa di Sant' Elia	PRINCE MILDRED	Newbury (d-h) (chase)	M. Scudamore
Jan 29	Major H.S. Cayzer	RENDEZ VOUS III	Kempton Park (chase)	M. Scudamore
Feb 18	Contessa di Sant' Elia	*PRINCE MILDRED	Hurst Park (chase)	M. Scudamore
Mar 7	Contessa di Sant' Elia	SARAH'S BOY	Newbury (hurdle)	F. Winter
Mar 20	Col. M.J. Gilliat	ROYAL TOURNAMENT	Wincanton (chase)	B. Lawrence
Apr 8	T.T. Jasper	OSCAR WILDE	Chepstow (chase)	B. Lawrence
Apr 12	Miss F.M. Prior	DROVER'S WAY	Hurst Park	S. Clayton
Apr 18	Lord Hampden	OURAGAN	Newbury	D. Smith
Apr 21	E.R. Rickman	ROXBURGH	Alexandra Park	D. Smith

Chronological List of Winners

Apr 25	Mrs. G.B. Hunt	PHOENIX PARK	Sandown Park	M. Hayes
	Mrs. M.D. Herniman	ROSE KNIGHT	Sandown Park	W. Rickaby
June 2	E.B. Baring	PENULTIMATE	Lewes	K. Wright
June 12	Brigadier H.R. Harris	GOLDEN THREAD	Brighton	M. Hayes
June 28	Mrs. B. Skipwith-Tyser	MERSEY PILOT	Alexandra Park	T. Carter
July 1	E.R. Rickman	ROXBURGH	Brighton	M. Hayes
July 8	E.B. Baring	PENULTIMATE	Salisbury	S. Clayton
July 11	Contessa di Sant' Elia	PNEUMATIC	Sandown Park	D. Smith
July 16	Mrs. N. Stuart-Cuff	PING CHING	Bath	J. Lindley
Aug 14	Lord Hampden	OURAGAN	Bath	J. Mercer
Aug 28	Mrs. N. Stuart-Cuff	PING CHING	Brighton	J. Lindley
Sept 19	Brigadier H.R. Harris	GOLDEN THREAD	Kempton Park (d-h)	P. Brownsea
Oct 23	Contessa di Sant' Elia	PNEUMATIC	Newbury	D. Smith
Oct 25	Miss F.M. Prior	ROGATION DAY	Newbury	W. Rickaby
Nov 14	Col. M.J. Gilliat	ROYAL TOURNAMENT	Cheltenham (chase)	R.E. Jenkins
Nov 22	T.T. Jasper	OSCAR WILDE	Sandown Park (chase)	R.E. Jenkins

1959

Feb 16	T.T. Jasper	OSCAR WILDE	Birmingham (chase)	R.E. Jenkins
Mar 25	C.W.F. Pudge	ST. ANTHONY	Worcester (chase)	R.E. Jenkins
Apr 6	Contessa di Sant' Elia	PRINCE MILDRED	Fontwell Park (chase)	Mr. J. Lawrence
Apr 24	Mrs. G.B. Hunt	PHOENIX PARK	Sandown Park	D.W. Morris
Apr 27	Miss F.M. Prior	AULD LANG SYNE	Worcester	D.W. Morris
May 2	Contessa di Sant' Elia	PNEUMATIC	Newmarket	D. Smith
May 9	D.E. Colebrook	PRETTY CAGE	Worcester	D. Keith
May 18	E.R. Rickman	ROXBURGH	Chepstow	F. Barlow
	Brigadier H.R. Harris	GOLDEN THREAD	Chepstow	S. Millbanks
May 20	D.E. Colebrook	PRETTY CAGE	Windsor	D. Keith
May 21	Major H.S. Cayzer	DELPH	Windsor	D. Keith
June 1	Mrs. N. Stuart-Cuff	LI KIN	Lewes	D. Greening
June 27	D.E. Colebrook	PRETTY CAGE	Lingfield Park	W. Rickaby
	Miss F.M. Prior	ROGATION DAY	Lingfield Park	W. Snaith
July 13	E.R. Rickman	ROXBURGH	Alexandra Park	R.P. Elliot
Aug 4	D.E. Colebrook	PRETTY CAGE	Brighton	D. Keith
Aug 6	Miss F.M. Prior	MEAD	Brighton	L. Piggott
Aug 22	Brigadier H.R. Harris	GOLDEN THREAD	Lingfield Park	S. Millbanks
	Mrs. N. Stuart-Cuff	LI KIN	Lingfield Park	S. Millbanks
Aug 24	Mrs. C.H. Feilden	CARRICK LODGE	Worcester	D. Keith
Sept 4	E.R. Rickman	ROXBURGH	Hurst Park	R.P. Elliot
Oct 17	Contessa di Sant' Elia	PRINCE MILDRED	Fontwell Park (chase)	R.E. Jenkins
Nov 21	T.T. Jasper	OSCAR WILDE	Sandown Park (chase)	R.E. Jenkins
Nov 23	Mrs. J.M. Stephenson	HILARION	Fontwell Park (hurdle)	R.E. Jenkins

1960

Jan 8	Mrs. J.M. Stephenson	HILARION	Sandown Park (hurdle)	R.E. Jenkins
July 7	E.R. Rickman	COMMUTER	Salisbury	A. Breasley
July 21	E.R. Rickman	COMMUTER	Kempton Park (d-h)	A. Breasley
Aug 3	Major H.S. Cayzer	DELPH	Brighton	D.W. Morris

Months of Misery Moments of Bliss

Aug 9	G.R. Rickman	RENO	Alexandra Park	W. Rickaby
Aug 10	W.G.R. Wightman	PNEUMATIC	Sandown Park	D. Smith
Aug 11	E.R. Rickman	ROXBURGH	Bath	P. Brownsea
Aug 17	W.G.R. Wightman	CHILCOMBE BELLE	Salisbury	E. Grant
Aug 19	D.E. Colebrook	PRETTY CAGE	Lingfield Park	A. Breasley
Aug 24	T.T. Jasper	GAY MUSTANG	Brighton	W. Rickaby
Sept 7	Major H.S. Cayzer	DELPH	Folkestone	D. Smith
Sept 30	Mrs. N. Stuart-Cuff	ROXBURGH	Newbury	E. Grant
Oct 5	Major H.S. Cayzer	DELPH	Lingfield Park	E. Grant
Oct 7	W.G.R. Wightman	CHILCOMBE BELLE	Ascot-at-Kempton	E. Grant
Oct 8	Mrs. J.A. Cecil-Wright	KAIKOURA	Warwick	E. Smith
Oct 15	Mrs. J.A. Cecil-Wright	KAIKOURA	Wolverhampton	L. Piggott
Oct 20	Mrs. W.G.R. Wightman	PNEUMATIC	Newbury	D. Smith
Dec 15	Mrs. G.B. Hunt	PHOENIX PARK	Sandown Park	T. Pink

1961

Mar 6	Contessa di Sant' Elia	SARAH'S BOY	Worcester (hurdle)	T. Pink
Mar 16	Mrs. N. Stuart-Cuff	ROXBURGH	Lingfield Park (hurdle)	T. Pink
Apr 20	Contessa di Sant' Elia	PIPER	Wincanton (hurdle)	T. Pink
Apr 26	Contessa di Sant' Elia	PIPER	Fontwell Park (hurdle)	T. Pink
June 12	G.R. Rickman	RENO	Lewes	R.P. Elliot
Aug 19	Mrs. W.G.R. Wightman	PNEUMATIC	Newbury	R.P. Elliot
Sept 6	D.E. Colebrook	PRETTY CAGE	Lingfield Park	D. Keith
Oct 3	Mrs. P. Ramus	EYES DOWN	Nottingham	P. Tulk
Dec 2	Mrs. N. Stuart-Cuff	ROXBURGH	Windsor (hurdle)	T. Pink

1962

Apr. 12	Mrs. W.G.R. Wightman	PANISSE	Taunton (chase)	M. Scudamore
May 17	J.S. Hughes	TANNHILLS	Salisbury	D. Keith
June 14	Major H.S. Cayzer	GREY SEAS	Brighton	J. Lindley
July 2	Mrs. H.S. Cayzer	GIFT ACCOUNT	Brighton	D. Smith
July 30	J.S. Hughes	TANNHILLS	Windsor	D. Keith
Aug 13	G.R. Rickman	HURUNUI	Folkestone	D. Keith
Aug 22	C.J. Devine	CRIMSON CONQUEST	Bath	W. Elliot
Sept 3	G.R. Rickman	BECKET	Windsor	J. Lindley
Sept 11	Mrs. N. Stuart-Cuff	ROXBURGH	Fontwell Park (hurdle)	T. Pink
Sept 12	S. Wingfield Digby	ELAN	Lingfield Park	D. Keith
Sept 17	Miss O.E. Hoole	ADORATION	Wolverhampton	D. Keith
	Mrs. N. Stuart-Cuff	ROXBURGH	Wolverhampton	D. Keith
Sept 21	C.J. Devine	CRIMSON CONQUEST	Kempton Park	J. Lindley
Sept 24	G.R. Rickman	BECKET	Windsor	J. Lindley
Sept 25	Major H.S. Cayzer	GREY SEAS	Leicester	D. Keith
Oct 3	T.T. Jasper	VALLEY ROCK	Fontwell Park (hurdle)	T. Pink
Oct 5	Mrs. H.S. Cayzer	GIFT ACCOUNT	Windsor	D.W. Morris

Chronological List of Winners

Oct 22	Brigadier H.R. Harris	TUDOR LIGHT	Birmingham		D. Keith
Nov 7	Mrs. N. Stuart-Cuff	ROXBURGH	Fontwell Park (hurdle)		T. Pink

1963

Apr 19	Miss F.M. Prior	RUNNYMEDE	Newbury	D. Keith
May 11	J.S. Hughes	TANNHILLS	Chepstow	E. Eldin
May 13	Mrs. W.G.R. Wightman	FRAXINUS	Brighton	D. Smith
May 23	Mrs. W.G.R. Wightman	FRAXINUS	Sandown Park	D. Keith
June 3	G.R. Rickman	BECKET	Birmingham	D. Ryan
June 12	Mrs. N. Stuart-Cuff	EYES DOWN	Brighton	D.W. Morris
June 26	Miss F.M. Prior	RUNNYMEDE	Newbury	D. Keith
June 28	Brigadier H.R. Harris	TUDOR LIGHT	Windsor	W.H. Carr
July 6	Brigadier H.R. Harris	TUDOR LIGHT	Lingfield Park	J. Mercer
July 15	Mrs. N. Stuart-Cuff	LING FING	Birmingham	D.W. Morris
	Mrs. H.S. Cayzer	GIFT ACCOUNT	Birmingham	D.W. Morris
	Mrs. N. Stuart-Cuff	EYES DOWN	Lewes	D. Keith
Aug 2	Mrs. W.G.R. Wightman	FRAXINUS	Goodwood	D. Yates
Aug 3	Major H.S. Cayzer	GREY·SEAS	Warwick	R. Fawdon
Aug 5	T.T. Jasper	VALLEY ROCK	Chepstow	W.H. Carr
Sept 14	Miss F.M. Prior	RUNNYMEDE	Newbury	D. Keith
Sept 19	E.R. Rickman	ROEDEAN	Yarmouth	D. Cullen
Sept 23	Mrs. J.A. Thomson	HUGOR	Windsor	D. Yates
Sept 25	Major H.S. Cayzer	GOLD GALORE	Pontefract	D. Keith
Sept 26	Mrs. P. Ramus	CONVALLARIA	Pontefract	D. Keith
Oct 14	Mrs. N. Stuart-Cuff	LING FING	Wolverhampton	B. Mills
Oct 21	Mrs. N. Stuart-Cuff	ROXBURGH	Birmingham	D.W. Morris
Nov 20	M.W. Tufnell	BADBURY RINGS	Kempton Park (chase)	T. Pink

1964

May 14	J.S. Hughes	TANNHILLS	Salisbury	D. Keith
May 19	Miss F.M. Prior	RUNNYMEDE	Sandown Park	D. Keith
May 20	Mrs. H.S. Cayzer	CHOPINIANA	Bath	G. Starkey
May 26	Mrs. H.S. Cayzer	CHOPINIANA	Alexandra Park	D. Keith
May 26	Mrs. N. Stuart-Cuff	EYES DOWN	Alexandra Park	D. Keith
May 29	J.S. Hughes	TANNHILLS	Newbury	M. Ginn
May 30	W.G.R. Wightman	FRAXINUS	Newbury	D. Yates
June 2	Mrs. N. Stuart-Cuff	ROXBURGH	Epsom	R. Hutchinson
June 13	W.H. Benham	DIRECTORY	Sandown Park	D. Yates
July 1	Mrs. H.S. Cayzer	GIFT ACCOUNT	Salisbury	H. Grattan
July 2	Mrs. W.I. Stirland	COURTERANI	Salisbury	A. Breasley
July 15	Mrs. W.I. Stirland	COURTERANI	Yarmouth	D. Smith
July 29	E.B. Baring	UNPREDICTABLE	Goodwood	G. Starkey
Aug 5	W.G.R. Wightman	FRAXINUS	Brighton	D. Yates
Oct 22	E.K. Cross	LING FING	Newbury	M. Thomas

1965

Mar 25	Major H.S. Cayzer	TUELLERAMA	Warwick	M. Thomas
Apr 12	Mrs. G.B. Hunt	ZUGELA	Alexandra Park	D. Keith

Months of Misery Moments of Bliss

Apr 13	M.W. Tufnell	BADBURY RINGS	Fontwell Park (chase)	O. McNally
Apr 23	Miss F.M. Prior	ABERYSTWYTH	Sandown Park	R.P. Elliot
Apr 28	Miss F.M. Prior	RUNNYMEDE	Newmarket	D. Keith
May 7	W.H. Benham	DIRECTORY	Kempton Park	R. Hutchinson
May 17	A.E. Bullen	ISIS	Brighton	A. Breasley
May 19	Mrs. N. Stuart-Cuff	EYES DOWN	Folkestone	M. Thomas
June 23	Mrs. N. Stuart-Cuff	EYES DOWN	Newbury	M. Ginn
June 29	J.D. Morgan	SINGER	Brighton	D. East
July 2	Major H.S. Cayzer	HALLUCINATION	Sandown Park	L. Piggott
July 21	Major H.S. Cayzer	TUELLERAMA	Bath	J. Mercer
Aug 5	Miss F.M. Prior	MEADOWSWEET TOO	Brighton	R. Hutchinson
Aug 6	Major H.S. Cayzer	TUELLERAMA	Windsor	G. Lewis
Aug 11	Miss F.M. Prior	ABERYSTWYTH	Salisbury	M. Thomas
Aug 27	W.H. Benham	DIRECTORY	Goodwood	R.P. Elliot
Sept 4	Mrs. G.B. Hunt	ZUGELA	Sandown Park	P. Cook
Sept 9	W.H. Benham	IYELLA	Salisbury	R.P. Elliot
Sept 6	*M.W. Tufnell*	*BADBURY RINGS*	*Fontwell Park (chase)*	*P. Hedger*
Oct 12	*M.W. Tufnell*	*BADBURY RINGS*	*Fontwell Park (chase)*	*P. Hedger*
Nov 17	*M.W. Tufnell*	*BADBURY RINGS*	*Windsor (chase)*	*P. Hedger*

1966

Mar 25	Mrs. G. Marten	SPUNYARN	Lingfield Park	J. Lindley
Apr 2	W.G.R. Wightman	EYES DOWN	Ascot	G. McCann
Apr 21	J.D. Morgan	SINGER	Epsom	G. McCann
Apr 29	J.D. Morgan	SINGER	Ascot	G. McCann
June 9	A.E. Bullen	ISIS	Brighton	D. Keith
June 23	Mrs. H.S. Cayzer	GIFT ACCOUNT	Newbury	G. McCann
June 28	A.G. Samuel	REPRISE	Brighton	D. Keith
June 30	Mrs. H.S. Cayzer	FOUETTE	Salisbury	W. Carson
July 1	Mrs. G.B. Miller	FLOURISH	Bath	R.P. Elliot
July 2	A.G. Samuel	STICKY GREEN	Bath	D. Yates
July 16	A.E. Bullen	ISIS	Ascot	D. Keith
	Mrs. M.M. Anson	QUOODLE	Wolverhampton	R.P. Elliot
Aug 5	Mrs. H.S. Cayzer	FOUETTE	Windsor	A. Breasley
Aug 25	Miss F.M. Prior	MAYFLOWER TOO	Brighton	D. Keith
Aug 31	Mrs. G.B. Miller	FLOURISH	Lingfield Park	R. Hutchinson
Sept 5	Major H.S. Cayzer	TUELLERAMA	Warwick	L. Piggott
Sept 20	*M.W. Tufnell*	*BADBURY RINGS*	*Fontwell Park (chase)*	*O. McNally*
Oct 1	Mrs. H.S. Cayzer	FOUETTE	Windsor	J. Lynch
Oct 3	W.H. Benham	DIRECTORY	Newbury	M. Thomas
	M.W. Tufnell	*BADBURY RINGS*	*Wye (chase)*	*O. McNally*
Oct 21	A.E. Bullen	THE ADVOCATOR	Doncaster	M. Thomas
Oct 25	*M.W. Tufnell*	*BADBURY RINGS*	*Fontwell Park (chase)*	*O. McNally*

1967

Feb 9	Mrs. J.A. Thomson	DIOR	Wincanton (hurdle)	O. McNally
May 10	J.D. Morgan	JAVATA	Newbury	D. Keith
May 15	A.G. Samuel	TUMBLED ANNA	Brighton	B. Taylor

Chronological List of Winners

May 20	J.D. Morgan	JAVATA	Lingfield Park	D. Keith
May 27	Mrs. G. Marten	SPUNYARN	Kempton Park	M. Thomas
May 31	W.H. Benham	FRAXINUS	Brighton	D. Keith
June 16	W.H. Benham	FRAXINUS	Sandown Park	E. Johnson
June 19	E.B. Benjamin	THANE	Brighton	M. Thomas
July 7	Brigadier H.R. Harris	SWARDESTON	Chepstow	D. Keith
July 7	A.G. Samuel	TUMBLED ANNA	Chepstow	D. Keith
July 13	Miss F.M. Prior	PASTURAGE	Brighton	D. Keith
July 24	Miss F.M. Prior	SINGING VALLEY	Folkestone	D. Keith
July 27	Major W.D. Gibson	KINGDOM	Goodwood	D. Keith
Aug 2	E.B. Benjamin	THANE	Bath	D. Keith
Aug 3	Mrs. G.B. Miller	FLOURISH	Brighton	M. Thomas
	Mrs. P. Ramus	EYES DOWN	Brighton	M. Thomas
Aug 4	Mrs. M.G.D. Kell	ENRAPTURED	Chepstow	D. Keith
Aug 5	Mrs. N. Parr	BLUEIT	Chepstow	D. Keith
Aug 17	Mrs. N. Stuart-Cuff	DIRECTORY	Goodwood	E. Johnson
Sept 4	Mrs. M.G.D. Kell	ENRAPTURED	Warwick	M. Thomas
Sept 5	M.W. Tufnell	BADBURY RINGS	Fontwell Park *(chase)*	O. McNally
Nov 23	M.W. Tufnell	BADBURY RINGS	Kempton Park *(chase)*	O. McNally
Dec 2	Mrs. G. Marten	SPUNYARN	Saint-Cloud	Y. Saint-Martin

1968

Apr 6	Miss L. Poyser	MELODOR	Ascot	P. Tulk
Apr 26	W. Lowndes	SPUNYARN	Sandown Park	G. Lewis
June 3	E.B. Benjamin	CELEBRATION II	Sandown Park	M. Thomas
June 15	E.B. Benjamin	CELEBRATION II	Bath	A. Breasley
June 17	W.G.R. Wightman	GREY SMOKE	Leicester	D. Keith
July 4	D.E. Colebrook	PRIVATEER	Salisbury	J. Lindley
July 5	D.E. Colebrook	HARD TO KEEP	Bath	J. McKeown
July 9	Mrs. N. Parr	BLUEIT	Newmarket	W. Carson
July 20	Miss L. Poyser	MELODOR	Lingfield Park	D. Keith
July 25	Mrs. P. Ramus	EYES DOWN	Sandown Park	R. Hutchinson
July 25	Major W.D. Gibson	KINGDOM	Sandown Park	R. Hutchinson
Aug 8	Mrs. M.G.D. Kell	ENRAPTURED	Bath	W. Carson
Aug 14	Mrs. M.G.D. Kell	ENRAPTURED	Salisbury	D. Keith
Aug 19	Mrs. N. Parr	BLUEIT	Windsor	W. Carson
Sept 2	Mrs. W.D. Gibson	ADVENT	Wolverhampton	W. Carson
	M.W. Tufnell	DIRECTORY	Chepstow	R. Dicey
Sept 17	D.E. Colebrook	HARD TO KEEP	Yarmouth	M. Thomas
Sept 26	*Major H.S. Cayzer*	*HALLUCINATION*	*Wincanton (hurdle)*	*B. Lawrence*
Oct 21	W.G.R. Wightman	BROOKWAY	Leicester	W. Carson
Oct 26	Mrs. N. Parr	BLUEIT	Doncaster	W. Carson

1969

June 21	Major H.S. Cayzer	RADIANT PRINCESS	Brighton	B. Jago
June 27	Mrs. W.D. Gibson	KINGDOM	Kempton Park	R. Hutchinson
July 2	Mrs. N. Parr	BLUEIT	Salisbury	B. Jago
July 9	Mrs. F. Phelps-Penry	TACITA	Brighton	G. Lewis

Months of Misery Moments of Bliss

July 12	E.B. Benjamin	BAREBACK	Newbury	E. Hide
	E.B. Benjamin	HIERARCH	Brighton	G. Starkey
July 14	D.E. Colebrook	PRIVATEER	Windsor	E. Hide
July 18	Major W.D. Gibson	THANE	Lingfield Park	B. Jago
July 21	Major H.S. Cayzer	RADIANT PRINCESS	Windsor	D. Greening
	D.E. Colebrook	PRIVATEER	Leicester	E. Hide
July 25	Miss L. Poyser	MELODOR	Ascot	E. Hide
July 26	Major W.D. Gibson	THANE	Ascot	B. Jago
	Mrs. G.B. Hunt	BILLY STRONG	Warwick	E. Hide
Aug 4	D.E. Colebrook	HARD TO KEEP	Wolverhampton	W. Carson
Aug 7	Mrs. G.B. Hunt	BILLY STRONG	Pontefract	E. Hide
Aug 12	Major H.S. Cayzer	RADIANT PRINCESS	Windsor	B. Jago
Aug 15	Mrs. M.G.D. Kell	ENRAPTURED	Newbury	M. Hurn
Aug 20	Major H.S. Cayzer	PREDESTINATION	Goodwood	E. Hide
Aug 22	D.E. Colebrook	HARD TO KEEP	Lingfield Park	B. Jago
Aug 27	D.E. Colebrook	HARD TO KEEP	Yarmouth	B. Jago
Aug 30	M.W. Tufnell	DIRECTORY	Windsor	E. Hide
	W.G. Lowndes	TRACKLECKA	Bath	E. Hide
Sept 11	M.N. Tufnell	BROOKWAY	Doncaster	W. Carson
Sept 20	Miss L. Poyser	MELODOR	Kempton Park	E. Hide

1970

Mar 13	Mrs .W.D. Gibson	*KINGDOM*	*Sandown Park (hurdle)*	*G. Dartnall*
May 30	E.B. Benjamin	OUR NOTE	Newbury	E. Hide
June 2	Major W.D. Gibson	THANE	Salisbury	W. Carson
June 10	E.B. Benjamin	OUR NOTE	Kempton Park	D. Keith
	E.B. Benjamin	HIERARCH	Kempton Park	D. Cullen
June 13	Mrs. W.D. Gibson	DOUANE	Sandown Park	A. Cousins
June 15	Capt. F. Barker	RALLY DRIVER	Brighton	R. Hutchinson
June 26	Mrs. M.G.D. Kell	ENRAPTURED	Chepstow	E. Hide
July 21	Mrs. M.G.D. Kell	ENRAPTURED	Alexandra Park	W. Carson
July 30	E.B. Benjamin	OUR NOTE	Goodwood	E. Hide .
Aug 6	D.E. Colebrook	PRIVATEER	Brighton	W. Carson
Aug 8	W.G. Lowndes	TRACKLECKA	Newmarket	B. Taylor
Aug 12	Mrs. W.D. Gibson	KINGDOM	Salisbury	E. Hide
Aug 18	Major W.D. Gibson	THANE	Folkestone	E. Hide
Oct 12	W.G.R. Wightman	UP AND AWAY	Warwick	E. Hide

1971

May 24	Miss D. Terry	PC'S RECORD	Windsor	F. Morby
May 26	Mrs. M.N. Tufnell	SOURIS	Brighton	B. Jago
June 30	D.E. Colebrook	PRIVATEER	Salisbury	F. Morby
July 2	Mrs. W.D. Gibson	DOUANE	Sandown Park	M. Thomas
Aug 5	D.E. Colebrook	PRIVATEER	Brighton	M. Thomas
Aug 20	Sir Derek Vestey	BLUE WARRIOR	Lingfield Park	J. Lindley
Oct 19	Mrs. J.A. Thomson	QUEEN'S FASHION	Sandown Park	E. Hide
Oct 26	Mrs. J.A. Thomson	LIMELIGHT	Nottingham	E. Hide

Chronological List of Winners

1972

July 6	D.E. Colebrook	PRIVATEER	Newmarket	W. Carson
July 18	Mrs. W.D. Gibson	QUEENDOM	Leicester	W. Carson
July 27	Mrs. W.D. Gibson	QUEENDOM	Goodwood	W. Carson
Aug 7	Sir Derek Vestey	MAJOR TORY	Nottingham	W. Carson
Aug 25	Mrs. M. Pakenham	PLONK	Goodwood	W. Carson
Aug 28	Lady Nichola Boyle	CYCLAMATE	Wolverhampton	J. Mercer
Sept 7	M. Pakenham	SOMERSWAY	Salisbury	G. Baxter
Sept 8	D.E. Colebrook	PRIVATEER	Doncaster	E. Hide
Sept 18	B. O'Neill	CATHY JANE	Bath	J. Mercer
Sept 19	Mrs. W.D. Gibson	QUEENDOM	Lingfield Park	W. Carson

1973

Mar 26	D.M. McKellar	WESTWARD LEADING	Leicester	E. Hide
Apr 3	Sir Derek Vestey	FABERGETTE	Nottingham	E. Hide
May 26	Major H.S. Cayzer	IMPORT	Newbury	G. Starkey
June 9	Mrs. W.D. Gibson	QUEENDOM	Epsom	W. Carson
June 12	Mrs. M. Pakenham	PLONK	Lingfield Park	W. Carson
June 23	S. Wingfield Digby	FLYING NELLY	Warwick	J. Mercer
June 29	S. Wingfield Digby	FLYING NELLY	Lingfield Park	W. Carson
	B. O'Neill	CATHY JANE	Lingfield Park	W. Carson
June 30	Mrs. W.D. Gibson	QUEENDOM	Lingfield Park	J. Wilson
July 11	Major H.S. Cayzer	IMPORT	Kempton Park	G. Starkey
July 28	B. O'Neill	CATHY JANE	Ascot	W. Carson
Aug 9	Miss D. Terry	DOUBLE RUM	Warwick	G. Starkey
Aug 11	Mrs. G.B. Miller	MIGHTIER YET	Haydock Park	J. Wilson
Aug 22	Mrs. W.D. Gibson	KINGDOM	Brighton	B. Taylor
Sept 1	Mrs. W.D. Gibson	QUEENDOM	Chester	W. Carson
Sept 18	M. Channon	CATHY JANE	Goodwood	C. Leonard
Sept 28	S. Wingfield Digby	FLYING NELLY	Ascot	G. Baxter
Oct 2	J.A. Leavett-Shenley	MISS BUBBLY	Nottingham	G. Baxter
Oct 6	T. Parrington	SOMERSWAY	Newmarket	D. Cullen
Oct 15	W.G.R. Wightman	LITTLE CHARTER	Warwick	E. Hide

1974

June 1	T. Parrington	SOMERSWAY	Kempton Park	D. Cullen
	Sir Derek Vestey	FABERGETTE	Kempton Park	G. Ramshaw
June 12	Mrs. F. Fleetwood-Hesketh	WALK BY	Newbury	M. Thomas
	Major H.S. Cayzer	IMPORT	Newbury	M. Thomas
July 6	S. Wingfield Digby	FLYING NELLY	Sandown Park	M. Thomas
July 27	T. Parrington	SOMERSWAY	Newcastle	A. Kimberley
Aug 5	D.E. Colebrook	KINGSCLERE	Folkestone	M. Thomas
Sept 2	D.E. Colebrook	KINGSCLERE	Warwick	P. Eddery
Sept 11	D.M. McKellar	WESTWARD LEADING	Salisbury	D. Cullen
Sept 12	Mrs. F. Fleetwood-Hesketh	WALK BY	Salisbury	D. Cullen
Sept 20	T. Parrington	SOMERSWAY	Ayr	D. Cullen
Sept 24	Miss D. Terry	THE GOLDSTONE	Leicester	E. Hide

Months of Misery Moments of Bliss

Oct 2	Major W.D. Gibson	BADESSA	Newmarket	M. Thomas
Oct 5	S. Wingfield Digby	FLYING NELLY	Newmarket	L. Maitland
Oct 7	E.B. Benjamin	GREAT LAD	Wolverhampton	M. Thomas
	D.M. McKellar	WESTWARD LEADING	Wolverhampton	D. Cullen
Oct 14	Lt.-Col. K. Mackessack	DUCK BUSTER	Warwick	M. Thomas
Oct 25	Lt.-Col. K. Mackessack	DUCK BUSTER	Newbury	M. Thomas
Nov 12	Miss D. Terry	KINDRED SPIRIT	Haydock Park	E. Hide
Nov 13	Mrs. H. Edwards	MODOM	Haydock Park	M. Thomas

1975

Mar 31	Mrs. G. Neal	SINGING TIME	Warwick	D. Cullen
Apr 25	S. Wingfield Digby	FLYING NELLY	Sandown Park	M Thomas
Apr 28	Mrs. H. Edwards	MODOM	Warwick	M. Thomas
June 10	Major H.S. Cayzer	IMPORT	Lingfield Park	J. Mercer
June 11	Mrs. F. Fleetwood-Hesketh	SOLAR	Newbury	G. Baxter
June 14	T. Parrington	SOMERSWAY	Sandown Park	D. Cullen
July 1	W.G.R.Wightman	BELL-TENT	Warwick	P. Eddery
	Mrs. G. Neal	SINGING TIME	Warwick	G. Baxter
July 5	Mrs. M.G.D. Kell	STARLIT WAY	Bath	T. O'Sullivan
July 14	W.G.R. Wightman	BELL-TENT	Leicester	T. O'Sullivan
July 29	Major H.S. Cayzer	IMPORT	Goodwood	M. Thomas
Aug 5	Mrs. J. A. Thomson	FLYING COLOURS	Brighton	D. Cullen
Aug 23	J. Morton	JETADOR	Newmarket	E. Eldin
Aug 26	J. Morton	JETADOR	Epsom	B. Jago
Sept 2	W.G.R. Wightman	BELL-TENT	Brighton	P. Eddery
Sept 11	Mrs. F. Fleetwood-Hesketh	SOLAR	Salisbury	G. Baxter
Sept 12	Mrs. F. Fleetwood-Hesketh	WALK BY	Doncaster	E. Hide
Sept 22	Mrs. G. Neal	RAFFIA SET	Bath	G. Baxter
Sept 29	Mrs. B. Thompson	WESTWARD LEADING	Nottingham	E. Hide
Oct 7	Mrs. G. Neal	RAFFIA SET	Brighton	G. Baxter
Oct 16	T. Parrington	SOMERSWAY	Newmarket	E. Hide
Oct 21	Brigadier H.R. Harris	WELCOME HONEY	Leicester	T. O'Sullivan
	Mrs. H. Edwards	MODOM	Chepstow	G. Baxter
	Mrs. S. Pakenham	THE GOLDSTONE	Chepstow	G. Baxter
Oct 24	E.B. Benjamin	GREAT LAD	Newbury	T. O'Sullivan
Oct 30	J. Morton	JETADOR	Newmarket	E. Eldin
Nov 3	Sir Derek Vestey	WINDMILL BOY	Leicester	E. Hide
Nov 4	Mrs. S. Pakenham	THE GOLDSTONE	Leicester	E. Hide
Nov 11	Miss D. Roth	CATAMARAN	Haydock Park	T. O'Sullivan

1976

May 25	W.G.R. Wightman	BELL-TENT	Salisbury	P. Eddery
May 29	Major H.S. Cayzer	IMPORT	Kempton Park	M. Thomas
May 31	W.G.R. Wightman	BELL-TENT	Chepstow	A. Murray
June 11	W.G.R. Wightman	BELL-TENT	Sandown Park	M. Thomas
June 18	Major H.S. Cayzer	IMPORT	Royal Ascot	M. Thomas
June 21	Metair Freight Ltd.	METAIR	Brighton	W. Carson

Chronological List of Winners

June 29	S. Wingfield Digby	AIR TROOPER	Nottingham	M. Thomas
	J. Morton	JETADOR	Nottingham	M. Thomas
July 10	Metair Freight Ltd.	METAIR	Salisbury	G. Baxter
	S. Wingfield Digby	AIR TROOPER	Salisbury	D. Cullen
July 16	Mrs. F. Fleetwood-Hesketh	SOLAR	Newbury	G. Baxter
Aug 4	Lady Nichola Boyle	CYCLAMATE	Brighton	M. Thomas
	Mrs. J.A. Thomson	DIORINA	Brighton	M. Thomas
Aug 28	Mrs. S. Pakenham	THE GOLDSTONE	Goodwood	Miss Joy Penn
Sept 3	Mrs. S. Pakenham	THE GOLDSTONE	Sandown Park	G. Baxter
Sept 9	Metair Freight Ltd.	METAIR	Salisbury	M. Thomas
Sept 30	Metair Freight Ltd.	METAIR	Newmarket	M. Thomas
	Lady Scott	RHEOLA	Newmarket	L. Piggott

1977

Apr 9	S. Wingfield Digby	AIR TROOPER	Kempton Park	M. Thomas
Apr 16	S. Wingfield Digby	AIR TROOPER	Newbury	M. Thomas
Apr 22	S. Wingfield Digby	AIR TROOPER	Sandown Park	W. Carson
May 30	W.G.R. Wightman	BELL-TENT	Lingfield Park	P. Eddery
	O.N. Pike	METAIR	Lingfield Park	P. Eddery
June 7	Major H.S. Cayzer	QUICK RETORT	Chepstow	D. Cullen
June 21	Miss K. Clarke	PARK WALK	Brighton	P. Eddery
June 22	W.G.R. Wightman	BELL-TENT	Salisbury	P. Eddery
June 30	Mrs. S. Pakenham	THE GOLDSTONE	Brighton	P. Eddery
July 1	S. Wingfield Digby	AIR TROOPER	Sandown Park	M. Thomas
July 8	Major H.S. Cayzer	QUICK RETORT	Lingfield Park	P. Eddery
July 9	S. Wingfield Digby	AIR TROOPER	York	M. Thomas
July 15	O.N. Pike	METAIR	Newbury	M. Thomas
July 16	Mrs. F. Fleetwood-Hesketh	SMARTEN UP	Newbury	M. Thomas
	W.G.R. Wightman	BELL-TENT	Newbury	P. Eddery
July 25	Mrs. J. Orpen	CAPTAIN'S BEAUTY	Nottingham	E. Hide
Aug 6	Lady Scott	DEEPWATER BLUES	Lingfield Park	M. Thomas
Aug 11	F. Drury	ST. ANTHONY	Salisbury	P. Eddery
Aug 16	Mrs. J. Orpen	CAPTAIN'S BEAUTY	Folkestone	M. Thomas
Aug 17	O.N. Pike	METAIR	York	M. Thomas
Aug 20	Mrs. S. Pakenham	THE GOLDSTONE	Nottingham	M. Thomas
Sept 5	W.G.R. Wightman	DEEPWATER BLUES	Windsor	P. Eddery
Sept 9	Greenwood Electronics	MALLABEE	Doncaster	E. Hide
Oct 1	W. Douglas-Home	GOBLIN	Newmarket	L. Piggott
Oct 12	Mrs. J. Orpen	CAPTAIN'S BEAUTY	Haydock Park	E. Hide
Oct 18	Mrs. S. Pakenham	THE GOLDSTONE	Sandown Park	G. Baxter
Oct 20	A.G. Samuel	COLLECTOR'S DREAM	Wolverhampton	M. Thomas
	Richard Green	CHARLOTTE'S CHOICE	Wolverhampton	M. Thomas
Oct 31	D.W. Hill	ROTA	Leicester	M. Thomas

Months of Misery Moments of Bliss

1978

Mar 28	K.P. Dudfield	SOMERS HEIR	Warwick	M. Thomas
Apr 24	K.P. Dudfield	SOMERS HEIR	Warwick	M. Thomas
May 20	Richard Green	CHARLOTTE'S CHOICE	Newbury	M. Roberts
	Major H.S. Cayzer	KING ALFRED	Newbury	E. Johnson
May 29	Mrs. R.B Kennard	SMARTEN UP	Sandown Park (d-h)	M. Thomas
May 30	Major H.S. Cayzer	KING ALFRED	Chepstow	J. Reid
June 2	Mrs. G. Neal	RAFFIA SET	Kempton Park	G. Starkey
June 7	W.G.R. Wightman	BELL-TENT	Epsom	P. Eddery
June 8	Richard Green	CHARLOTTE'S CHOICE	Epsom	M. Thomas
June 9	J.A. Peterswald	COURAGEOUS KING	Haydock Park	P. Eddery
June 12	Mrs. A.S. Kinnear	SANDOR	Lingfield Park	M. Thomas
June 21	S. Wingfield Digby	KNIGHTS MOVE	Beverley	S. Woolley
June 30	Mrs. S. Pakenham	THE GOLDSTONE	Lingfield Park	G. Baxter
July 10	J.A. Leavett-Shenley	GOLDEN MOET	Windsor	G. Baxter
July 27	Mrs. S. Pakenham	THE GOLDSTONE	Goodwood	G. Baxter
Aug 2	K.P. Dudfield	SOMERS HEIR	Brighton	B. Rouse
Aug 19	D.B. Clark	SAUCY MELODY	Nottingham	S. Woolley
Aug 25	G. Martin	ARDTULLY LASS	Goodwood	S. Woolley
Aug 29	W. Kelly	QUEEN'S NIECE	Chepstow	P. Eddery
Sept 13	Richard Green	CHARLOTTE'S CHOICE	Doncaster	W. Carson
Sept 14	Mrs. S. Pakenham	THE GOLDSTONE	Salisbury	Karen Wiltshire
Oct 4	W. Douglas-Home	GOBLIN	Brighton	P. Waldron
Oct 18	M. Channon	MAN ON THE RUN	Folkestone	P. Eddery
Oct 20	W. Douglas-Home	GOBLIN	Lingfield Park	G. Baxter
Oct 27	S. Green	AVON SALMON	Newbury	A. Bond
Oct 30	Richard Green	JAMES WARD	Chepstow	S. Woolley
Nov 6	Sir Derek Vestey	SONG OF GOLD	Leicester	S. Woolley

1979

May 9	Richard Green	CHARLOTTE'S CHOICE	Chester	W. Carson
June 1	Sir Derek Vestey	SONG OF GOLD	Kempton Park	W. Carson
June 14	Mrs. A.S. Kinnear	SANDOR	Newbury	R. Newman
July 28	Lady Scott	QUITE RIGHT	Warwick	R. Curant
Aug 17	J. Hughes Farms Ltd.	SWEET AS A NUT	Newbury	S. Woolley
Aug 21	W. Douglas-Home	GOBLIN	Folkestone	R. Curant
Aug 22	H.E. Waller	DAFYDD	Brighton (d-h)	R. Curant
Aug 29	S. Wingfield Digby	NELLY DO DA	Bath	F. Morby
Aug 31	T. Parrington	WEARMOUTH	Sandown Park	J. Mercer
Sept 14	Lady Georgina Coleridge	ROCKAWAY	Goodwood at Sandown	J. Mercer
Oct 2	Mrs. Basil Samuel	COUNT CARLOS	Newbury	J. Mercer
Oct 4	W. Douglas-Home	GOBLIN	Newmarket	G. Baxter
Oct 8	M. Channon	MAN ON THE RUN	Bath	W. Newnes
Oct 18	W. Kelly	QUEEN'S NIECE	Haydock Park	W. Newnes

Chronological List of Winners

Oct 25	K.P. Dudfield	SOMERS HEIR	Wolverhampton	W. Newnes
Nov 5	D.B. Clark	KING'S RIDE	Leicester	P. Eddery
Nov 8	D.B. Clark	KING'S RIDE	Teesside Park	E. Hide

1980

Feb 13	Mrs. S. Pakenham	THE GOLDSTONE	Ascot (hurdle)	M. Reeves
Mar 22	D.B. Clark	KING'S RIDE	Doncaster	G. Baxter
Mar 29	G. Martin & Co. Ltd.	MARSTAIN	Salisbury	G. Baxter
May 8	Mrs. R.B. Kennard	ASHBRITTLE	Salisbury	S. Woolley
June 7	Mrs. R.B. Kennard	ASHBRITTLE	Epsom	G. Starkey
June 25	T. Parrington	WEARMOUTH	Salisbury	J. Mercer
June 27	Mrs. J.M. Joyce	XARFINA	Lingfield Park	S. Woolley
July 4	D.B. Clark	KING'S RIDE	Haydock Park	E. Hide
Aug 8	Mrs. J.M. Joyce	XARFINA	Haydock Park	S. Salmon
Aug 19	Lady Scott	PILLAR TO POST	Folkestone	B. Taylor
Aug 26	Richard Green	QUEEN'S EQUERRY	Epsom	L. Piggott
Sept 5	Major H.S. Cayzer	ADMIRAL'S BARGE	Haydock Park	P. Eddery
Sept 6	D.B. Clark	KING'S RIDE	Kempton Park	M. Thomas
Sept 8	Mrs. R.B. Kennard	ASHBRITTLE	Windsor	G. Starkey
Nov 7	Major H.S. Cayzer	BANBURY CROSS	Doncaster	G. Starkey

1981

Mar 30	Mrs. S. Pakenham	THE GOLDSTONE	Leicester	K. Butler
Apr 27	A.G. Samuel	CORVEN	Brighton	W. Carson
June 10	Richard Green	CHARLOTTE'S CHOICE	Newbury	S. Woolley
Aug 6	Richard Green	QUEEN'S EQUERRY	Brighton	W. Newnes
Aug 22	Richard Green	CHARLOTTE'S CHOICE	Chester	B. Taylor
Aug 26	Mrs. J.A. Thomson	CHERI BERRY	Bath	E. Johnson
Aug 31	Mrs. J.A. Thomson	CHERI BERRY	Epsom	R. Curant
Sept 3	Richard Green	CHARLOTTE'S CHOICE	York	P. Cook
Sept 7	R.H. Till	LUCKY LOVE	Windsor	B. Rouse
Sept 14	J.A. Peterswald	SIR SAMUEL	Goodwood	G. Baxter
Sept 22	D.B. Clark	KING'S RIDE	Lingfield Park	G. Baxter
Sept 28	Miss D. Roth	NINEVEH	Nottingham	G. Baxter
Oct 2	Lt.-Col. W.E.S. Wetherly	SOUND OF THE SEA	Lingfield Park	R. Curant
Oct 22	Mrs. S.D. Maxwell	TELEGRAPH BOY	Wolverhampton	E. Johnson

1982

June 21	Miss D. Downes	INCHGOWER	Brighton	S. Salmon
July 17	J.R. Brown	ROMAN RULER	Nottingham	R. Fox
July 26	Miss D. Downes	INCHGOWER	Windsor	S. Salmon
Aug 25	Miss D. Downes	INCHGOWER	Brighton	S. Salmon

Months of Misery Moments of Bliss

Sept 16	Lt.-Col. W.E.S. Wetherly	SOUND OF THE SEA	Brighton	W. Newnes
Sept 21	P. Bridge	HANABI	Leicester	D. McKay
Oct 11	Miss H. Stratton	SWEET ECSTASY	Warwick	P. Eddery
Oct 25	Mrs. J.A. Thomson	CHERI BERRY	Nottingham	G. Baxter
Oct 30	Miss H. Stratton	SWEET ECSTASY	Newmarket	W. Newnes

1983

May 5	Mrs. R.B. Kennard	HARBOUR BRIDGE	Salisbury	B. Rouse
May 31	Miss D. Downes	INCHGOWER	Leicester	B. Rouse
	J.R. Brown	ROMAN RULER	Leicester	G. Duffield
June 30	Miss D. Downes	INCHGOWER	Brighton	B. Rouse
July 29	Mrs. A. Norman	SOUND OF THE SEA	Goodwood	G. Baxter
Aug 4	J.R. Brown	ROMAN RULER	Brighton	B. Rouse
Aug 10	Mrs. R.B. Kennard	CUTLERS CORNER	Salisbury	G. Starkey
Aug 20	Mrs. A. Norman	SOUND OF THE SEA	Sandown Park	T. Quinn
Sept 26	Mrs. M.M. Hunt	IT'S A PLEASURE	Nottingham	W.R. Swinburn
Oct 4	Mrs. J.A. Thomson	CHERI BERRY	Wolverhampton	W. Newnes
Oct 20	Mrs. J.A. Thomson	CHERI BERRY	Newbury	T. Quinn
Nov 17	*Miss D. Downes*	*INCHGOWER*	*Kempton Park (hurdle)*	*M. Harrington*

1984

June 16	A.G Lansley	SINGLE	Bath	D. McKay
June 28	Miss D. Downes	INCHGOWER	Salisbury	Mr. T. Thomson Jones
Aug 18	Mrs. A. Norman	SOUND OF THE SEA	Newbury	S. Whitworth
Aug 22	Mrs. R.B. Kennard	CUTLERS CORNER	York	S. Cauthen
Aug 30	Miss D. Downes	INCHGOWER	Brighton	B. Rouse
Sept 24	Mrs. R.B. Kennard	LA TUERTA	Bath	G. Starkey
Sept 26	Mrs. A. Norman	SOUND OF THE SEA	Sandown Park	S. Whitworth
Oct 5	Mrs. R.B. Kennard	CUTLERS CORNER	Newmarket	S. Cauthen

1985

May 18	A.G. Lansley	SINGLE	Newbury	D. Eddery
May 28	Miss D. Downes	INCHGOWER	Leicester	B. Rouse
July 29	A.G. Lansley	SINGLE	Bath	D. McKay
Oct 23	*Mrs. D. Downes*	*INCHGOWER*	*Cheltenham (hurdle)*	*P. Scudamore*

1986

Apr 10	A.G. Lansley	SINGLE	Chepstow	P. Eddery
Apr 22	A.G. Lansley	SINGLE	Epsom	D. Eddery
May 2	*Miss Jill Pelly*	*MAJOR TOM*	*Plumpton (chase)*	*M. Harrington*
May 8	A.G. Lansley	SINGLE	Salisbury	D. McKay
Sept 2	*Mrs. J.A. Thomson*	*DISPORT*	*Fontwell Park (hurdle)*	*M. Harrington*

Chronological List of Winners

1987
Mar 21	Mrs. R. Newton	FORMIDABLE LADY	Lingfield Park (hurdle)	S Smith Eccles
Apr 27	T.R. Mountain	SEGOVIAN	Brighton	G. French
June 12	A.G. Lansley	SINGLE	Chepstow	P. Eddery
July 18	A.G. Lansley	SINGLE	Newbury	P. Eddery
Aug 5	T.R. Mountain	SEGOVIAN	Brighton	R. Fox
Aug 12	A.G. Lansley	SINGLE	Salisbury	P. Eddery
Sept 18	A.G. Lansley	SINGLE	Newbury	P. Eddery
Sept 24	A.G. Lansley	SINGLE	Ascot	P. Eddery
Dec 18	N.J. Hitchins	POPESWOOD	Lingfield Park (hurdle)	I. Shoemark

1988
May 9	W.G.R. Wightman	PRIOK	Windsor	M. Thomas
June 23	D.B. Clark	MARTINOSKY	Salisbury	M. Thomas
Aug 16	Mrs. R. Newton	DIVINE PET	Folkestone	B. Rouse

1989
Mar 9	N.J. Hitchins	POPESWOOD	Wincanton (hurdle)	R. Dunwoody
Mar 13	W.G.R. Wightman	OUT YONDER	Plumpton (hurdle)	M. Richards
Mar 27	N.J. Hitchins	POPESWOOD	Wincanton (hurdle)	R. Dunwoody
May 15	D.B. Clark	MARTINOSKY	Windsor	W. Carson
May 23	Mrs. A. Norman	DIVINE PET	Salisbury	B. Rouse
June 16	T.R. Mountain	STAR HILL	Goodwood	J. Williams
July 15	T.R. Mountain	STAR HILL	Lingfield Park	J. Williams
July 27	T.R. Mountain	STAR HILL	Goodwood	J. Willams
Aug 3	Mrs. A.J. Taylor	DIVINE PET	Brighton	R. Fox
Aug 12	Mrs. A.J. Taylor	DIVINE PET	Newbury	B. Rouse
Sept 2	T.R. Mountain	STAR HILL	Kempton Park	J. Williams
Oct 11	J.A. Leavett-Shenley	KINGSBROOK	Plumpton (chase)	J. Railton

1990
July 5	D.B. Clark	MARTINOSKY	Brighton	J. Williams
Oct 22	Mrs. R. Newton	GOLDEN BIRCH	Folkestone	J. Williams
Nov 3	Mrs. R. Newton	GOLDEN BIRCH	Newmarket	W. Carson

1991
Feb 5	W.G.R. Wightman	INSWINGER	Lingfield Park (AW)	Mr. G. Killie
Mar 11	N.J. Hitchins	POPESWOOD	Plumpton (chase)	M. Richards
Aug 8	Mrs. A.J. Taylor	DIVINE PET	Brighton	Tyrone Williams
Aug 17	Mrs. A.J. Taylor	DIVINE PET	Newbury	Tyrone Williams

1992
Mar 21	Mrs. J.M. Joyce	GREAT HALL	Lingfield Park (AW)	J. Williams
Apr 22	A.G. Lansley	GOOGLY	Folkestone	G. Bardwell
May 4	A.G. Lansley	GOOGLY	Kempton Park	G. Bardwell
May 30	D.B. Clark	MARTINOSKY	Lingfield Park	J. Williams
June 26	Mrs. J.A. Thomson	HALLORINA	Goodwood	G. Bardwell
June 29	Mrs. J.A Thomson	MARDIOR	Windsor	G. Carter

Months of Misery Moments of Bliss

July 16	Mrs. J.A. Thomson	HALLORINA	Chepstow	G. Bardwell
	D.B. Clark	MARTINOSKY	Chepstow	J. Williams
July 25	W.G.R. Wightman	INSWINGER	Southwell (AW)	G. Bardwell
July 30	Mrs. J.A. Thomson	HALLORINA	Goodwood	G. Bardwell
Aug 13	A.G. Lansley	GOOGLY	Salisbury	G. Bardwell
Sept 3	T.R. Mountain	CATHERINEOFARAGON	Salisbury	J. Williams
Sept 14	Mrs. A.J. Taylor	DIVINE PET	Bath	J. Williams
Sept 25	A.G. Lansley	GOOGLY	Haydock Park	G. Bardwell

1993

May 3	*W.G.R. Wightman*	*IN THE ZONE*	*Fontwell Park (chase)*	*P. Hobbs*
May 8	Mrs. J.A. Thomson	HALLORINA	Bath	G. Bardwell
May 17	Mrs. J.A. Thomson	HALLORINA	Bath	G. Bardwell
July 29	A.G. Lansley	GOOGLY	Goodwood	J. Reid
Oct 21	A.G. Lansley	GOOGLY	Newbury	J. Reid